RECIPES

Hyperac

RECIPES FOR HEALTH

Hyperactive Child

Over 150 recipes to help hyperactivity and other food intolerances

JANET ASH & DULCIE ROBERTS

Thorsons
An Imprint of HarperCollinsPublishers

Thorsons
An Imprint of HarperCollins*Publishers*
77–85 Fulham Palace Road,
Hammersmith, London W6 8JB

1160 Battery Street,
San Francisco, California 94111–1213

First published by Thorsons 1986 as
Happiness is Junk-Free Food
Revised edition published 1990
This edition revised and updated 1996

1   3   5   7   9   10   8   6   4   2

A catalogue record for this book
is available from the British Library

ISBN 0 7225 3292 X

Typeset by Harper Phototypesetters Limited,
Northampton, England
Printed and bound in Great Britain by
Caledonian International Book Manufacturing Ltd, Glasgow

Contents

Foreword

RECIPES FOR HEALTH: The Hyperactive Child is a long-needed book to help mothers of problematic children.

The field of nutritional medicine is expanding at a tremendous rate and public demand for this type of medicine is far outstripping the medical profession's willingness to embrace a non-toxic, nutritional approach to the management of illness; instead, it seems to prefer the more toxic drug prescribing approach.

Thus, there is a need for sensible books of this type to help parents care for their children in a way that does not involve drugging or simply ignoring the problem.

This book provides a host of recipes avoiding 'junk' food. Any diet that concentrates on fresh unprocessed foods, de-emphasizing those foods containing chemical additives and refined sugar and flour, is a diet which will inevitably be healthier than the usual British diet.

The authors are to be congratulated on the work that they have put into producing such a useful book.

T. Stephen Davies M.A., B.Ch.
Medical Advisor to the Hyperactive Children's Support Group

Acknowledgements

W E WOULD like to thank most sincerely all those who have helped us to compile this recipe book.

Our very special thanks to those who have so generously allowed us to reprint or adapt their recipes. Also, we would like to thank Mrs I. D. Colquhoun and Sally Bunday, Founders of the Hyperactive Children's Support Group, on behalf of all the many families who have been helped by their dedication and devotion.

With many thanks to Hanne Parkhouse BSc Hons SRD for all her work on the nutritional assessment of the menu guide.

Very sincere appreciation to Ron, Nigel and friends for their patience, understanding and assistance.

Introduction

THIS RECIPE book has been compiled for hyperactive children. It is important that it should accompany the Hyperactive Children's Support Group Diet Handbook *Hyperactive Children: A Guide to their Management* so that readers have full information on the subject.

The recipes are based on the Feingold Diet. Dr Ben Feingold was an American allergist who observed that children who were sensitive to aspirin also showed hyperactivity, which was improved by a salicylate (aspirin)-free diet (some fruits and vegetables contain natural salicylate which is closely allied in basic structure to aspirin). He then went on to observe that, in sensitive children, substances unrelated to aspirin, such as artificial food colours, flavours and preservatives, could cause the same reactions. In the light of these findings he formulated a diet to exclude all artificial colours, flavours and preservatives and, for the first four to six weeks, naturally occurring salicylates. Dr Feingold wanted to help these children without the use of drugs which may have potentially harmful side-effects, hence the Feingold Diet.

Over the years there has been criticism levelled against the Feingold Diet. There have been trials claiming that it does not work and denies the child the pleasures of 'ordinary' foods. However, the Feingold Diet is based on healthy foods and therefore does provide a nourishing diet. Often a diet that is high in convenience, highly processed foods provides empty calories stripped of their vitamins and minerals; for example, a packet of crisps provides calories but not the goodness of a baked potato.

Some of the trials which set out to disprove the Feingold Diet, using double-blind methods, tested only a small part of the Feingold programme; for example, testing the elimination of some artificial colours but still giving artificial flavours, preservatives and salicylates. They then stated that the Feingold Diet did not work.

However, recent studies in Britain confirmed the adverse effects of artificial colours on hyperactive children. They also found that some children reacted to cow's milk, chocolate, orange and wheat. For this reason we have included some milk-free and wheat-free recipes (indicated as such at the top of recipes concerned). It is important to stress that eliminating wheat or milk from the diet must only be done on the advice of your doctor or State Registered Dietitian.

It must also be recognized that there is conflicting evidence on the amounts of salicylates in foods and the effects they may have. Indeed, some authorities do not advocate the elimination of salicylates from the diet for this reason. However, the Hyperactive Children's Support Group and the experience of many parents suggests that, even though foods containing salicylates are wholesome, they can cause adverse reactions in those sensitive to them.

After four to six weeks of the diet, the improvement in symptoms should be noted and then those fruits and vegetables containing natural salicylates should be reintroduced into the child's diet, one at a time, so that any offending variety can be identified and eliminated. Full instructions are provided in the Hyperactive Children's Support Group Diet Handbook.

Certain herbs and spices contain high levels of salicylates, but as they are only used in small amounts, they may be tolerated. We have asterisked (*) in the recipes those which could cause problems for children who are hypersensitive.

The greatest success is observed when the whole family keeps to the diet which is based on healthy eating. When the offending foods are not available in the house there is less risk or temptation for the hyperactive child.

HELPFUL HINTS

When you start the diet, remember to read labels on everything you buy. If ingredients are not listed or if you are unsure about an ingredient then the food is best avoided. Manufacturers are continually changing the ingredients in their products. So always be alert.

Keep a guess what? box of allowed treats, permitted fruit, nut bars, etc. Let the child dip into this.

Food and drink. Take some food and drink out with you

on short and long trips. Hyperactive children use up a lot of energy and need plenty of between-meal healthy snacks, such as fresh and dried fruit, nut bars and sandwiches. Very often a 'whiny' child will be better after a drink and/or snack. This will also stop you from buying the 'wrong food', and help you stick to the diet. Remember, even a mouthful of wrong food can cause a reaction. The HACSG includes a safe food list with diet information for members. To improve and maintain optimum health it is better to eat wholefoods rather than refined foods which have had a lot of their goodness removed in processing. Aim to eat some raw fruit at each meal and one salad per day. Avoid all chemical additives in foods. You will be amazed how much better you will feel and look, also how much energy you have. The better our health, the less likely we are to be ill. We also have more resistance to disease, allergies, and pollutants in the atmosphere. By eating foods as near to their natural state as possible, you are also feeding the body with vitamins and minerals in their natural state so that imbalances do not occur. However, a sudden change to a wholefood diet can cause excessive bowel movements, therefore organic white and 85 per cent flours may be kinder to children's digestive systems initially.

Sugar

Sugar consumption is generally too high for our own good. Reports suggest that over 72lb (approx 33 kg) per person per year is eaten. Most processed foods (even savoury and vegetable foods) have sugar and salt added to them and both are very often added in cooking and again in serving. As a diet high in sugar is related to tooth decay and may aggravate hyperactivity, it is a good idea to cut down consumption of sugar in any form. A lot of parents report further improvements in their children after gradually reducing sugar in their diet, especially by cutting down on fizzy, sugary drinks and sweets which can take away the appetite for more nourishing foods.

Greater consumption of sugar, white or brown, means inferior nutrition, because sugar provides 'empty calories' that have been stripped of minerals and vitamins. Sugar occurs naturally in fruits and some vegetables, which also contain vitamins, minerals and fibre lacking in refined sugars.

You may find some of our recipes are not sweet enough for you – yet!!! Gradually reduce the amount of sugar you use. After a while it will become quite natural to use smaller quantities.

All starchy foods, such as bread, cereals, potatoes, rice and pasta, should provide our main energy needs. These foods also contain B vitamins and fibre, particularly the wholemeal and wholegrain varieties.

Natural Food Flavours and Colours

These are available from most health food shops and some supermarkets.

Baking Powder

To make your own use one part bicarbonate of soda

(baking soda) to two parts cream of tartar. See page 189 for recipe.

Arrowroot, Tapioca and Sago

These are recommended for people suffering from food allergies, but have little nutritional value. Millet (obtainable whole, flaked or as a flour) is better.

Uncooked Egg White

Destroys biotin, one of the B vitamins. Avidin in the white latches on to biotin, making it unavailable to the body.

Sulphur Dioxide

Wash dried fruits well in boiling water to remove some of the sulphur dioxide. Rinse well in cold water. Caution: sulphites E220–E228 can cause adverse reactions in asthmatics.

Lemon, Pineapple or Grapefruit Juice

Use any of these juices to preserve the colour of cut pieces of fruit, e.g. pear or banana.

Permitted Stewed Fruit Juices

Strain any extra juice and use as a drink, or mix with other permitted fruit juices. Call drinks 'fruit cocktails'. Add a slice of lemon and ice cubes for extra interest.

Tea and Coffee

These are stimulants. To wean your child off them, make permitted drinks in a small teapot. It will be fun for the child to pour out his/her own 'special drink'. See drink section on pages 264–74.

Chocolate

Even pure additive-free cocoa contains caffeine and theobromine which are stimulants. Use carob as a chocolate substitute.

Oils Recommended

The best oils to use for salad dressings are safflower or sunflower which are high in essential fatty acids. Use cold-pressed oils as these have not gone through a heat treated process using chemicals to bleach and deodorize them. Although expensive, unrefined oils are much healthier. Eicosapentaenoic (EPA) is an essential fatty acid found in oils, coming from fatty fish such as herrings, mackerel, sprats, salmon and sardines.

A school of thought says it is not good to use highly polyunsaturated oils such as safflower or sunflower for frying as they can cause dangerous particles called free radicals to be released, which may accelerate the ageing process, particularly if there is no vitamin E present. Probably the best oils to use for cooking are olive or sesame, or a little butter. If you use margarine or other oils, make sure they have a vitamin E added.

Frying

Keep to a minimum – grill instead.

Malt

Is suspect. So look out for malt flavouring, especially in breakfast cereals if these upset the child.

Canned Foods

Do not store food or drinks in their cans.

Dill and Fennel (Herbs)

Have a sweet flavour. Will help to cut down the amount of sugar used. Obtainable at health food stores.

To Toast Nuts

Spread out on a baking sheet and put in a moderate oven for approx. ten minutes.

Hazelnuts

Not usually necessary to skin, but if desired, prepare as for toasted nuts and keep in oven for approx. 20 minutes. Rub off skins with a clean tea towel or kitchen paper.

Freezing

If you own a freezer you will not miss convenience foods so much if you:
1. Make large batches of burgers, rissoles, fish, cakes, stews, soups, main meals, etc.
2. Cook double quantities of pulses and whole brown rice. Freeze in small amounts. You will soon have a variety which you can use in salads and stews, etc.

Pressure Cooker

Is a marvellous cooking aid especially for pulses which take from 10–30 minutes depending on variety, or whole brown rice which takes approx. 15 minutes.

Food Flask

Useful for 'any time meals', packed lunches, travelling or even at home.

Salad Spinner

A must – spins washed salads dry in seconds.

Recipe Books

To keep clean when in use, place open book in a clear polythene (plastic) bag.

Vegetables

Try and buy fresh vegetables, organically grown if possible, and which have not been on display outside shops where they can collect lead fumes from petrol. Try and steam vegetables, cook using a simple steaming basket. The flavour is much better and the vitamins are not so easily lost. Use the water you have cooked vegetables in for gravies, soups, stews, etc. It contains a lot of nutrients. Cook vegetables without salt. They have salt naturally occurring in them.

Labels

Read labels and see how many times salt and sugar are added to processed food.

Eggs

Buy free-range eggs. The taste and texture, even the smell, are completely different.

Washing Fruit and Vegetables

Remember to wash all fruit and vegetables before use. Scrub skins of citrus fruit. These may have been dyed.

Saucepans

Try and use stainless steel saucepans instead of aluminium ones.

Perseverence

Keep persevering with the diet. Even a small amount of 'wrong' food may cause a reaction.

Overcooking

It is better not to overcook food, especially vegetables, as all the vitamins will be lost into the water.

Green potatoes

Avoid, as they contain a poisonous alkaloid, solanin. Also avoid potatoes with blight.

Fruit Drinks

These are not pure fruit juices so do not buy them.

Seasonings

It is better for small children not to have highly spiced

foods and it is a good idea to cut down on salt and pepper. While a little salt is very necessary to us, too much is not and can be very harmful. Many processed foods seem to have salt and sugar added to them. Salt occurs naturally in vegetables and need not be added in cooking.

Certain herbs and spices contain high levels of salicylates, but as they are only used in small amounts, they may be tolerated.

HYPERACTIVE CHILDREN'S SUPPORT GROUP

For Hyperactive, Allergic and Learning Disabled Children.

Aims of the Group

A. The relief of children who are in need of care and attention by reason of being handicapped through hyperactivity.
B. To conduct research and promote investigation into the incidence of hyperactivity in the U.K., its causes and treatments; and to disseminate information concerning this condition.

About the Hyperactive Children's Support Group

The Hyperactive Children's Support Group was founded in November 1977 and grew into a national association almost overnight. The group was granted charitable status in May 1979, Registered Charity

277643. The Group is not in receipt of any Government Grants or Loans. The only financial support comes from members' subscriptions, outside donations and the sale of literature.

The Group supplies information on dietary therapy and other forms of help and treatment. Newsletters keep members, both lay and professional, up to date with latest research and other important data.

Hyperactive children are often allergic (intolerant of some foods and chemicals) and learning disabled because they are not able to concentrate. These children have a very short attention span, even though they may be bright and intelligent (see pages 13–14 for symptoms).

We ask for open minds on the subject of the dietary approaches to this multiple handicap as an alternative to drug based therapy. The Group cannot offer individual medical advice as NO MEMBER HAS ANY MEDICAL QUALIFICATIONS. However, the Group has medical advisers and is in touch with various hospitals and doctors who are willing to help. Professional enquiries welcome. For full information write to HACSG, Sally Bunday, 71 Whyke Lane, Chichester, West Sussex, PO19 2LD, enclosing a 23cm x 10cm stamped self-addressed envelope. (The HACSG is a voluntary organization. In any correspondence PLEASE SEND A STAMPED ADDRESSED ENVELOPE OR STAMPS TO COVER.)

SYMPTOMS AND DESCRIPTIVE CHARACTERISTICS

Not every child will have all the symptoms and these will be in varying degrees.

In Infancy

Crying, screaming, restlessness – needing very little sleep.
Colic – very difficult to feed whether breast or bottle fed.
Cannot be pacified or cuddled – often spurns affection.
Excessive dribbling – may be very thirsty.
Fits and tantrums.
May not crawl.

In Older Children (in addition to the above)

Clumsy, impulsive – often accident prone.
Erratic, disruptive behaviour.
Compulsive touching – everything and everyone.
Constant motion – wriggles legs.
May walk on toes – runs everywhere.
Disturbs other children – may be aggressive.
Unable to concentrate – never finish anything they
  begin.
Demands must be met immediately. Frustration leads
  to temper tantrums. Normal or high I.Q. but fails
  at school.
Poor appetite – poor hand and eye co-ordination.
Unco-operative – defiant and disobedient.
Self-abusive (pulling hair, picking skin, etc).

Continued problems with sleep – wakes many times in the night.

Cannot sit through a meal.

Many hyperactive children also suffer speech, hearing, vision and memory defects.

Other health problems include infantile colic, eczema, asthma, hay fever, rhinitis, and repeated chest and ear infections.

DETAILS OF DIET

This cookery book is based on the 'food programme' formulated by the late Dr Ben Feingold M.D., an American allergist, who spent many years researching the possibility of chemical food additives being linked to hyperactivity and behavioural disturbances. His aim was to get children better without causing harm – i.e. using diet in the management of hyperactivity as an alternative to drugs.

Two groups of food are eliminated by this diet.

Group 1

All food and drink containing synthetic COLOURING and FLAVOURING are forbidden. Also Monosodium Glutamate, Sodium Glutamate, Nitrite, Nitrate, Butylated Hydroxytoluene (B.H.T.), Butylated Hydroxyanisole (B.H.A.) used as anti-oxidants, sodium benzoate, benzoic acid and artificially sweetened products.

Group 2

To be omitted for 4–6 weeks: certain fruits and vegetables containing naturally occurring 'salicylates' to which these children may be sensitive. (See glossary on salicylates.) For information on reintroducing these foods after 4–6 weeks, see the HACSG Handbook.

Not Permitted

Almonds
Apples (also cider and
    cider vinegar)
Apricots
All berries (Bilberries,
    blackberries,
    boysenberries,
    strawberries,
    raspberries, gooseber-
    ries, elderberries, and
    dewberries)
Cherries
Cloves
Coffee
Cola
Corn

Cucumbers, gherkins
    and pickles
Currants, grapes and
    raisins (also wine
    and wine vinegar)
All peppers and chillies
Mint
Nectarines
Oranges
Peaches
Plums and prunes
Tangerines
Tea
Tomatoes
Oil of Wintergreen

Because of the elimination of these fruit and vegetables, it is important for the children to get sufficient vitamin C and although there are many other sources in the permitted fruit and vegetables as listed below the Group can advise on extra vitamin supplements.

Permitted Fruit

Avocados
Bananas
Dates*
Figs
Grapefruit
Guavas
Lemons
Limes
Loquats

Mangoes
All melons
Papaya
Pears
Persimmon (Sharon fruit)
Pineapple*
Pomegranate
Rhubarb

Permitted Vegetables

Artichokes
Asparagus
Bamboo shoots
Beans (all except broad
    beans)
Bean sprouts
Broccoli
Brussels sprouts
Cabbage
Calabrese
Carrots
Cauliflower
Celery
Celeriac
Chard
Chicory*
Chinese leaves

Chives
Cress
Collard Greens
Fennel
Leeks
Kale
Kohlrabi
Lettuce
Lentils
Marrow (summer squash)
Mushroom (not canned)
Okra
Onions
Parsley
Parsnip
Peas
Potatoes

Radish (red and white)	Squash
Shallots	Swede (rutabaga)
Spinach	Sweet potato
Spring greens	Turnip
Spring onions (scallions)	Watercress

Permitted

All seeds and nuts *except* Almonds

Pulses

(Whole not split are best)	Haricot beans
Aduki beans	(navy beans)
Black eye beans	Kidney beans
Butter beans (Lima beans)	Lentils
Canellini beans	Mung beans
Chickpeas (garbanzo	Borlotti beans
beans)	(pinto beans)
Flageolet beans	Soya beans (soy beans)

In cases of extreme salicylate sensitivity Dr Feingold recommended the elimination of other salicylate-containing foods, these being potatoes, bananas, coffee, pineapple, and all sources of benzoates (see Glossary). Benzoate occurs naturally in cranberries and peas and is also used frequently as a preservative e.g. sodium benzoate, benzoate of soda, etc. Other salicylate-containing fruits not on the Feingold list are tamarind, passion fruit, olive, peppermint and mint.

Despite extensive enquiries it is proving difficult to

ascertain accurate details on amounts of salicylates contained in foods. You may need to test each fruit and vegetable separately.

The willow tree was the original source of pain-killing medicines made from salicylates and the leaves, bark, fruits, flowers and stems of willow and the following plants contain salicylates:

acacia	camelia	poplar	violet
aspen	hyacinth	spirea	
birch	marigold	teaberry	
calcanthus	milkwort	tulip	

OTHER FACTORS AFFECTING HYPERACTIVITY

There are a number of chemical or environmental hazards which may also affect you or your child.

In the Home

1. Aerosols, such as spray polishes, window, pan, oven or shoe cleaners.
2. Insecticides.
3. Felt tipped pens.
4. Newsprint.
5. Air fresheners.
6. Perfumes, hair sprays, coloured bubble baths and toothpastes.
7. Avoid synthetic fabrics, such as polyester. Natural fabrics are better. Be wary of dry cleaning,

waterproofing and moth-proofing etc.

8. Washing powders, particularly the types containing enzymes. Clothes washed in any detergent should be well rinsed. Some can cause severe irritation and eczema.

9. Washing up liquid. Dishes should be rinsed in hot water.

10. Paint and varnish fumes.

11. Natural gas, coal fires and paraffin heaters may affect some children.

12. Animal fur.

13. House dust.

14. Tap water. This contains chlorine, and possibly fluoride which may affect some children and adults.

Environmental Hazards

1. Swimming baths. The chlorine affects many children, particularly hyperactive ones.

2. Diesel fumes, petrol fumes, formaldehyde fumes from modern furnishings and carpets.

3. Glues and other industrial solvents.

4. Foods. Apart from the artificial colourings, flavourings, preservatives, etc., which are added to our foods, many poisonous sprays, insecticides and herbicides are put on to it while it is growing. Chemicals are also sprayed on to fruit to prevent it from ripening too soon, or it can be dyed to make it look riper than it is.

5. Many farm animals are raised in factory conditions but free-range meats are now much more widely

available from farm shops and certain supermarkets.

6. Heavy metals

a) *Lead*. This is extremely toxic and affects the nervous system. Children and the unborn child are particularly susceptible.

Sources

1. Petrol.
2. Old paint. Children may chew this. Avoid dry sanding old lead paint, as the lead can be inhaled.
3. Drinking water. Leached from old lead pipes, more likely in soft water areas.
4. Road dust.

b) *Cadmium* – from cigarette smoking, or inhaling smoke while someone is smoking.

c) *Aluminium*

1. Aluminium saucepans, kitchen foil and foil cooking containers.
2. Some baking powders.
3. Deodorants

Toxic levels of lead, cadmium, aluminium and copper, or deficiencies of essential minerals such as calcium, iron, magnesium and zinc can have an adverse affect on health and may increase hyperactivity.

FOOD ALLERGIES OR INTOLERANCES

The following are some likely foods which may cause reaction in the most likely order of severity:

Chocolate	Sugar
Cow's milk	Tomato
Orange	Egg
Wheat	Pork
Cheese	Corn

A rotation diet will help to track these down.

WARNING. If you suspect your child is allergic to cow's milk, it is essential to seek medical advice. It is very important to be properly diagnosed before eliminating milk and milk products from the diet. Once a child is taken off cow's milk it is very dangerous to put a child back on it again, especially infants, without medical help.

Sedatives – Sedatives can have a reverse affect on hyperactive children. Ask your physician or pharmacist to prescribe non-coloured, non-flavoured drugs and medicines.

All the following products are available at health food stores. Remember to read all labels carefully.

GLUTEN-FREE FLOURS

Gluten is a substance found in wheat, rye, barley and oats. People with 'coeliac' disease cannot absorb the protein gluten in these grains. (For more information on coeliac disease, see page 276.) However some people with a wheat intolerance may be able to tolerate oats and barley, while others can tolerate wheat if it has been

organically grown, i.e. not treated with pesticides. Grains
that may be used as flours are:

MAIZE (CORNMEAL)	RICE FLOUR
MILLET FLOUR	BUCKWHEAT FLOUR

GRAIN-FREE FLOURS

CHICK PEA (GARBANZO) FLOUR. Also known as besan
or gram flour.
LIMA BEAN FLOUR. Also known as butter bean, curry
bean or pole bean.
LENTIL FLOUR
POTATO FLOUR. Also known as potato farina.
SOYA (SOY) FLOUR
SPLIT PEA FLOUR
ARROWROOT
SAGO
TAPIOCA
Although safe for a gluten-free diet, arrowroot, sago, and
tapioca are refined starches providing energy but hardly
any essential nutrients. It is better to use any of the above
flours.

COW'S MILK-FREE ALTERNATIVES

MILK FREE MARGARINE. Available from most health
food stores.
MILK. See page 265.
Soya (soy) milks or nut milks (see pages 23–4 and 265–6).
CHEESE. This may be tolerated by some, especially when

made with vegetable rennet, rather than calf rennet.

Goat's and Sheep's Cheeses. See pages 237–8.

YOGURT. (This may be tolerated.)

Goat's and sheep's yogurt available from health food stores and some supermarkets.

SOYA (soy) yogurts available mainly from health food stores.

EGG-FREE DIETS

Egg replacer is available at health food stores and from some supermarkets.

SOYA (SOY) PRODUCTS

WARNING: Soya can provoke allergic/intolerant reactions, so it is advisable not to eat too much soya regularly.

Soya (Soy) Beans. Contains all eight essential amino acids which the body cannot manufacture, and is highest in nutritional value of all beans. The whole beans take longer to cook than most, although a pressure cooker reduces the time to to 25–30 minutes. As with all beans they must be cooked thoroughly. For cooking times see page 105.

Soya (Soy) Flour. Best bought pre-cooked.

Tofu or soya (Soy) bean curd is a good source of calcium.

Soya (Soy) Milk. See pages 265–6.

Soya Desserts. Also soya 'yogurts', ice cream substitute and soya based 'cheese'. Available from health shops and some supermarkets.

Soya (Soy) Sauce. Tamari is a natural soya (soy) sauce which contains little or no wheat. Use as a seasoning and to bring out the flavour in gravies, soups and stews.

Shoyu. A natural soya (soy) sauce which contains soya (soy) beans and wheat. Use as for tamari.

Miso. This is fermented soya (soy) bean in paste form. Use as for soya (soy) sauce.

Soya (soy) products are available from health food shops and some supermarkets.

IMPORTANT NOTES

1. Information and recipes regarding gluten-free, milk-free and egg-free diets are merely a guide to those who must follow these diets. *Full medical help is essential and must be followed.* With this in mind we hope these recipes prove helpful.
2. The codings at the top of each recipe will help you find your requirements quickly.
3. REMEMBER: Certain foods which claim to be safe for certain diets may not be tolerated by you!!

FURTHER INFORMATION

The blue diet booklet sent out by the HACSG contains a comprehensive safe food list and addresses of suppliers. The foods have been checked with manufacturers concerned. Additions and cancellations are published in the journal every four months. It always includes a reading list and directory of useful addresses.

Menu Guide

THIS MENU Guide is based on the recipes in this
book but there are plenty of other recipes and foods
that can be used.

The HACSG sends out a list of safe foods which have
been checked with manufacturers as being free from
additives. As previously stated, it is important to obtain
these details from the HACSG before trying the
Feingold Diet.

The Menu Guide averaged over the week provides a
daily approximate amount of the following nutrients:

Calcium	1000mg	15% Protein
Iron	11mg	34% Fat
Zinc	9mg	50% Carbohydrate
Vitamin C	65mg	

The amounts of vitamins and minerals are slightly above
recommended dietary reference values for children and
adults published by the Department of Health.

Teenage girls, because of menstruation, need plenty of
iron, and should be careful to eat at least two portions of

iron-containing foods each day. Good sources of iron are red meat, liver, egg yolk, pulses, beans, lentils and chick peas. To help absorb the iron in these foods, eat them with foods containing vitamin C, such as lemon, grape-fruit, lime, pineapple and salads.

Several studies have found that hyperactive children have a low intake of the mineral zinc. Good sources of zinc are meat, chicken (dark meat), liver, sea food and eggs. Smaller amounts are contained in cheese, beans, oatmeal and wholemeal bread.

The amount of energy needed by growing children varies with age. Younger children need smaller portions, whilst teenagers may need much larger amounts of energy-containing starchy foods, such as bread, potato, rice and pasta. These carbohydrate foods also contain important B vitamins, particularly the wholemeal and wholegrain varieties. Choose at least one starchy food at each meal.

	Monday	Tuesday	Wednesday	Thursday	Friday	Saturday	Sunday
Breakfast	Crunchy Muesli Yogurt Water to drink	½ grapefruit Toast with butter Barley Cup	Toast with butter and marmalade Banana and Lemon Health Drink	Alpine Breakfast Barley Cup	Grapefruit and Melon Refresher Drop scones Milk to drink	Porridge Toast with butter Barley Cup	French toast Drink
Mid-morning	Fresh pear Lemon and Lime drink	Flapjack Water to drink	Fresh pear Diluted pineapple juice with sparkling water	Slice of toast with Marmite Lemon Barley Water	Pear Water to drink	Hazelnut Milk Shake	
Lunch	Homemade soup Toast	Sandwiches with sardine paste and cress	Jacket potato Cottage cheese Carrot Salad Milk to drink	Cheesy Sausages Cress	Watercress Soup Herbed Cheese Bread	Slice of pizza Green salad Water to drink	Roast lamb with roast or boiled potatoes and sprouts or carrots Rice pudding Tinned mangoes
Mid-afternoon	Coconut Bar Water to drink	Fresh pear Limeade	Homemade biscuit Water to drink	Sticky Lime Cake Milk to drink	Sesame Thins with Hummus Hawaiian Quencher	Lemon Bun Diluted pear juice	
Evening meal	Turkey Casserole Potatoes Cauliflower Pineapple Cream Water to drink	Lemon Chicken Mashed potato Carrots Mango Meringue Pudding	Homemade beefburgers and coleslaw in roll Carob Ice Cream Water to drink	Baked Fish in Yogurt Sauce Rhubarb Jelly Water to drink	Nut Roast and mashed potato Green salad Butterscotch Bananas Water to drink	Tuna and Cod Fish Cakes with cabbage or swede Fruit Salad Water to drink	Mashed banana with yogurt Bread or toast with butter and permitted jam Carrot Cake
Supper	Banana sandwich Carob milk	Hot milk Drop scone	Allowed cereal with milk	Oatcake Fennel tea	Toast Drink	Yogurt Scone Carob milk	Allowed cereal with milk

1

Breakfasts

GRAPEFRUIT AND MELON REFRESHER

This is really good to start the day with, as there's lots of vitamin C in this recipe. Alternatively use it as a sweet.

Serves 6
Gluten Free   Milk Free   Egg Free

Metric/Imperial		American
1 small	melon	1 small
1	grapefruit, peeled	1
Juice of ½	lime	Juice of ½
	raw cane sugar to taste	
	(ground or moist)	

1. Cut the melon and grapefruit into cubes.
2. Add the juice and sugar and mix well. Serve topped with chopped hazelnuts, walnuts (English walnuts), desiccated coconut, or dates.

ALPINE BREAKFAST

Serves 3–4
Egg Free

Metric/Imperial		American
1	grapefruit, peeled and segmented	1
1	pear, peeled and chopped	1
30g/1oz	chopped dates* or figs	2 tbs
30g/1oz	nuts of choice (brazil, hazelnuts, [English] walnuts or grated coconut)	3 tbs
30g/1oz	porridge (rolled) oats or wheatgerm	¼ cup
1 tsp	raw cane sugar	1 tsp
140ml/¼ pint	natural (plain) yogurt	⅔ cup

1. Chop the grapefruit and place in a bowl.
2. Add the chopped pear to prevent it discolouring.
3. Mix the rest of the ingredients with the fruit.
4. If possible, leave in the refrigerator or a cool place for an hour before serving, or keep overnight in the refrigerator so that it will be ready for breakfast.

CRUNCHY MUESLI

You can buy your muesli base from health shops, or mix your own if you wish. This is usually made up of oats, wheat flakes, rye flakes or wheatgerm.

20 servings
Milk Free   Egg Free

Metric/Imperial		American
4 tbs	safflower or sunflower oil	4 tbs
3 tbs	raw cane sugar	3 tbs
1 tsp	natural vanilla essence (optional)	1 tsp
455g/1lb	muesli base	2 cups
55g/2oz	sesame seeds	½ cup
55g/2oz	sunflower seeds	½ cup
55g/2oz	hazelnuts, (English) walnuts or brazil nuts, chopped	½ cup

1. Heat the oil and sugar. Add the vanilla essence, muesli base, seeds and nuts.
2. Remove from the heat and stir well to coat. Spread the mixture in a baking tin and bake in oven at 375°F/ 190°C/gas mark 5 for 30 minutes. You have to stir it quite often to stop it burning on top.
3. Store in a covered jar. Serve with milk, yogurt, fresh or dried fruits.

SHIRRED EGGS

This makes a quick, nourishing snack which can be eaten at any time of day.

Serves 4

Metric/Imperial		American
	butter or margarine	
85g/3oz	cheese, grated	1 cup
4 slices	bread, buttered	4 slices
4	eggs	4
	sea salt and freshly ground pepper to taste	
	parsley, to garnish	

1. Grease a large, ovenproof dish with butter or margarine and sprinkle a little cheese over the bottom of the dish. This will help prevent bread sticking to the dish.
2. Lay the slices of bread side by side, buttered side face down in the dish. Break the eggs and place over each slice of bread. Sprinkle over the rest of the cheese, salt and pepper.
3. Bake for 12–15 minutes at 350°F/180°C/gas mark 4 until eggs have set.
4. To serve, lift out each slice and put on a warmed plate. Garnish with the parsley.

FRENCH TOAST

Serves 2

Metric/Imperial		*American*
1	free range egg	1
1 tbs	milk	1 tbs
	sea salt and freshly ground pepper to taste	
2 slices	wholemeal (wholewheat) bread	2 slices
	oil	

1. Beat the egg and milk together and season.
2. Dip the bread into the egg mixture, then fry in hot oil for a minute on each side until browned.

FRUITY BREAKFAST YOGURT

Serves 4
Gluten Free   Egg Free

Metric/Imperial		American
1	grapefruit, peeled, segmented and chopped	1
1 large	banana, sliced	1 large
¼ small	melon, cubed	¼ small
3–4	figs, chopped and strigged	3–4
140ml/¼ pint	natural (plain) yogurt	⅔ cup

Stir the fruit into the yogurt. Chill and serve with wholemeal (wholewheat) toast, or Cinnamon and Walnut Drop Scones (Pancakes) (see page 38).

Note to Cooks

Best eaten the same day.

YOGURT

Gluten Free   Egg Free

Try making your own, it's much cheaper, and easy once you get the hang of it. It is a wonderful health giving food.

1. Heat 570ml (1 pint/2½ cups) milk almost to the boil.
2. Allow to cool until you can keep your little finger in the milk for 10 seconds, comfortably.
3. Mix 2 tablespoons natural (plain) yogurt with a little of the milk to make a smooth mixture, then combine with the rest.
4. Leave covered with a tea cloth or in a jar with a loosely fitting cap, in a warm kitchen, airing cupboard or, in winter, on the mantelpiece over the fire. You need to provide a steady warmth.
5. Check in 3 to 8 hours to see if it has set. Then put in the refrigerator.

Alternatively, sterilize a flask by pouring boiling water into it and leaving for 5 minutes. A wide necked flask is easier to spoon the yogurt out of when set. *Do not fill the flask completely to the top, as you must leave room for the gases inside to expand.* Pour in the mixture, screw down and leave to set, usually for about 6 hours. For a thick set yogurt, stir a tablespoon of dried skimmed milk into the yogurt starter before adding the milk. To serve, you can just stir in some honey, and top with chopped walnuts (English walnuts) or hazelnuts. Add your own permitted fruit, such as pineapple, mashed banana, chopped, puréed or liquidized figs.

Hyperactive Child

SOYA (SOY) YOGURT

Gluten Free   Milk Free   Egg Free

To make yogurt from soya (soy) milk, you just follow the same procedure but only heat the milk until it rises from the pan, stirring all the time. To make a thicker yogurt, use some concentrated soya (soy) milk with the ordinary soya (soy) milk. Use a vegetarian starter available from most health shops.

TO MAKE YOUR CURD CHEESE

Gluten Free   Egg Free

Add ½ teaspoon salt to 570ml (1 pint/2½ cups) of the homemade yogurt. Pour into a piece of muslin and hang it overnight to drain. Add your own chopped chives, a little garlic or sage.

OATMEAL PORRIDGE

Metric/Imperial		*American*
850ml/1½ pints	water	3¾ cups
¼ level tsp	ground sea salt	¼ level tsp
115g/4oz	medium oatmeal	1 cup

1. Bring the water to the boil, add the salt, then gradually stir in the oatmeal.
2. Cover pan and simmer for 20 minutes. When cooked, add cinnamon or fresh fruit for extra flavour. Serve with milk, soya (soy) milk, or yogurt and raw cane sugar or honey. Makes a warming breakfast on a cold day.

WHOLE MILLET PORRIDGE

Serves 4
Gluten Free   Egg Free

Metric/Imperial		American
115g/4oz	whole millet	½ cup
850ml/1½ pints	boiling water	3¾ cups
pinch	sea salt	pinch

1. Cook together gently for 25–30 minutes, when millet should be soft and fluffy. Serve with milk or yogurt, raw cane sugar and allowed fruit of choice.

CINNAMON AND WALNUT DROP SCONES (PANCAKES)

Makes 12

Metric/Imperial		American
115g/4oz	85% wholemeal flour	1 cup
1½ tsp	baking powder	1½ tsp
pinch	sea salt	pinch
½ tsp	cinnamon*	½ tsp
1 tbs	raw cane sugar	1 tbs
2 tbs	oil	2 tbs
1	free range egg, beaten	1
140ml/¼ pint	milk	⅔ cup
55g/2oz	(English) walnuts, chopped finely	½ cup

1. Sift together the flour, baking powder, sea salt, cinnamon and sugar.
2. Make a well in the centre and add the oil and egg, then gradually add the milk and walnuts (English walnuts).
3. Lightly oil a frying pan or griddle (skillet).
4. Drop tablespoons of the mixture on to the griddle and cook for a minute or two until bubbles appear on the top. Turn over and cook the other side until golden brown.
5. Serve immediately with butter, cottage cheese or fromage frais.

PARSNIP OR SWEDE
(RUTABAGA) FRITTERS

These are good for breakfast on a cold morning if you
have the vegetables left over from the night before.

Makes 4 large, 8 small
Egg Free

Metric/Imperial		American
½kg/1lb	parsnips or swede (rutabaga)	1 pound
15g/½oz	unsalted butter or margarine	1¼ tbs
55g/2oz	85% flour	½ cup
	sea salt and freshly ground pepper	
1 tbs	oil	1 tbs

1. Boil the vegetable, then mash well.
2. Rub the fat into the flour and add to the parsnips or
   swede (rutabaga), with salt and pepper to taste. Mix
   well.
3. Heat the oil in a pan and drop spoonfuls of the mixture
   into it, and fry until golden brown.

Notes to Cooks

Serve with scrambled, poached or fried eggs and toast.
Swede (rutabaga) may make smaller fritters than the
parsnip.

BANANA AND LEMON HEALTH DRINK

A lovely, refreshing and filling drink.

Serves 4
Gluten Free   Egg Free

Metric/Imperial		American
285ml/½ pint	natural (plain) yogurt	1⅓ cup
2 large	bananas	2 large
3 tsp	lemon juice	3 tsp
1 tbs	raw cane sugar	1 tbs

1. Liquidize all the ingredients together until frothy. Serve with slices of wholemeal (wholewheat) toast and you have an instant nourishing breakfast.

HAZELNUT MILK SHAKE

Serves 4
Gluten Free   Egg Free

Metric/Imperial		American
285ml/½ pint	milk	1⅓ cups
55g/2oz	hazelnuts, finely ground	½ cup
2 tsp	raw cane sugar	2 tsp
1	fresh pear, peeled and cored	1

1. Liquidize all the ingredients together until smooth.
   This makes a delicious protein packed drink.

For more recipes for drinks, see pages 264–74. For milk-free recipe, use soya milk.

Soups

T HESE REALLY are easy to make, and are cheap, nourishing and tasty, particularly on a cold winter's day, served with chunks of bread and grated cheese. The key is to make a good stock. For vegetable stock just save the liquor strained from cooked vegetables. For a chicken or meat stock, put the chicken carcass, meat bones or trimmings into a large saucepan. Add an onion, carrot, 1–2 celery stalks and tops, sprigs of parsley and a bay leaf. Cover with cold water, then bring to the boil and simmer (not boil or it will go cloudy), for 3–4 hours. Strain and keep in the refrigerator. Use within two days or freeze.

EVERYTHING SOUP

Serves 4
Gluten Free   Milk Free   Egg Free

Metric/Imperial		American
1	onion	1
1	clove of garlic (optional)	1
	leaves of green vegetables	
	tops of leeks	
	stalk and leaves of celery	
	carrots	
	a potato etc. until you have	
	455g/1lb prepared	
	vegetables	
2 tsp	mixed herbs*	2 tsp
850ml/1½ pints	vegetable stock or water	3¾ cups
	sea salt and freshly ground	
	pepper to taste	

1. Chop the vegetables, then lightly oil a frying pan (skillet) and gently sauté chopped onion, and garlic if used, until soft.
2. Add rest of vegetables, herbs and stock or water to barely cover.
3. Simmer until cooked (about 20–30 minutes).
4. Put through blender, and season to taste. Reheat and enjoy. It's never the same twice! Will freeze.

CAULIFLOWER SOUP

Serves 4–5
Gluten Free   Egg Free

Metric/Imperial		American
1 medium-sized	cauliflower	1 medium-sized
1 small	onion, sliced	1 small
1 tbs	chopped parsley	1 tbs
1	bay leaf*	1
570ml/1 pint	stock	2½ cups
285ml/½ pint	milk	1⅓ cups
	sea salt and freshly ground pepper to taste	
1–2 tsp	lemon juice	1–2 tsp

1. Divide the cauliflower into florets and put into a large saucepan with the onion, parsley, bay leaf, stock, milk and seasoning. Cook gently for 10–15 minutes, until soft.
2. Remove the bay leaf, then liquidize. Squeeze a little lemon juice into the soup, and season again if necessary to taste. Will freeze.

Note to Cooks

If you do not wish to use milk, substitute with 285ml/½ pint (1⅓ cups) additional stock.

MINESTRONE

Serves 4–6
Gluten Free   Milk Free   Egg Free

Metric/Imperial		*American*
about 455g/ 1lb	mixed vegetables (onions, runner beans, leeks, turnips, celery or carrots)	about 1 pound
2 tbs	oil	2 tbs
1 clove	garlic	1 clove
115g/4oz	cooked kidney beans	⅔ cup
55g/2oz	long grain brown rice	⅓ cup
850ml/1½ pints	water or vegetable stock	3¾ cups
pinch	sage, oregano and marjoram*	pinch
	sea salt and freshly ground pepper	

1. Prepare the vegetables and chop into small pieces.
2. Sauté them in the oil with the crushed garlic for 10 minutes.
3. Add the beans, rice, water and stock, herbs and seasoning.
4. Bring to the boil and simmer for 30 minutes. Will freeze.

CARROT AND LEMON SOUP

Serves 4
Gluten Free   Milk Free   Egg Free

Metric/Imperial		American
455g/1lb	prepared vegetables (e.g. 1 onion, 2 sticks [stalks] of celery, 6 medium-sized carrots)	1 pound
1 tbs	oil	1 tbs
2 tsp	grated lemon rind	2 tsp
1 tbs	lemon juice	1 tbs
1	bay leaf*	1
850ml/1½ pints	stock or water	3¾ cups
	sea salt and freshly ground pepper to taste	
	chopped parsley to serve	

1. Chop onion, celery and carrots finely and sauté gently in oil until the vegetables begin to soften, about 5–10 minutes.
2. Add half of the grated lemon rind, the bay leaf and stock or water, and simmer for about 20 minutes, until cooked.
3. Liquidize, then add the rest of the lemon rind, and the lemon juice and seasoning to taste.
4. Serve sprinkled with chopped parsley. Will freeze.

WATERCRESS SOUP

This is also delicious served cold on a hot summer's day. Chill well before serving.

Serves 4
Gluten Free   Milk Free   Egg Free

Metric/Imperial		American
455g/1lb	prepared vegetables (e.g. 1 large potato, 1 medium turnip, 1 onion)	1 pound
1 tbs	chopped parsley	1 tbs
1 bunch of	medium-sized watercress	1 bunch of
1 tbs	oil	1 tbs
570ml/1 pint	vegetable stock	2½ cups
	sea salt and freshly ground pepper	
1 tsp	lemon juice	1 tsp

1. Peel the potato, turnip and onion, and chop finely. Wash the parsley and watercress, saving two or three sprigs of watercress to garnish, then chop finely.
2. Sauté the onion, turnip and potato in the oil for 3–5 minutes. Add the chopped watercress and parsley and stock. Season and simmer gently for 15 minutes until the vegetables are tender.
3. Liquidize, and add the remaining watercress leaves to garnish.

LEEK AND POTATO SOUP

Serves 4–5
Gluten Free   Milk Free   Egg Free

Metric/Imperial		American
1 tbs	oil	1 tbs
455g/1lb	leeks, trimmed, sliced and washed	1 pound
1 small	onion, skinned and chopped	1 small
225g/½lb	potatoes, peeled and sliced	½ pound
570ml/1 pint	vegetable stock	2½ cups
	sea salt and freshly ground pepper to taste	
	chopped chives to garnish	

1. Heat the oil in a large saucepan and sauté the onion and potato for 5 minutes, then add the leeks. Coat well with the oil, and continue to sauté gently for a further 2 minutes.
2. Add the stock and seasoning and bring to the boil. Cover and simmer for about 15–20 minutes until the vegetables are tender.
3. Cool the soup, then liquidize, or rub through a sieve. Reheat, sprinkle with chopped chives to garnish, and serve with chunks of wholemeal (wholewheat) bread.

3

Fish

FISH MAKE the quickest and most nourishing meals. White fish can be grilled on an oiled grill pan for 2–3 minutes on each side, or baked in the oven for 15–20 minutes. You can add more flavours by sprinkling the fish with sesame seeds, mixed herbs*, soya/tamari sauce, lemon juice, or chopped fennel. Just brush the fish with a little oil or lemon juice first to help the flavourings to stick.

Mackerel can be baked or grilled, it can be stuffed, or cooked with onion rings. Trout can be flavoured from the inside with herbs such as fennel.

Finnan haddock, if you can find it, has no artificial colour added. To cook, simply poach it by putting it in a large saucepan and covering for 4 minutes with boiling water or sauté in a little butter until cooked. Makes delicious kedgeree or pâté.

FISH FINGERS (FISH STICKS)

Milk Free

1. Use fairly thick coley fillets, as cod tends to disintegrate. Chill the fish thoroughly, as it is then easier to handle.
2. Cut into straight fingers, trimming the ends square. Dip into wholemeal (wholewheat) flour, then beaten egg and brown breadcrumbs.
3. Leave in the refrigerator for the coating to harden, for at least an hour.
4. Fry in oil. Will freeze.

Note to Cooks

If coley is unavailable, use other firm white fish.

TUNA AND COD FISH CAKES

Makes 8
Milk Free   Egg Free

Metric/Imperial		American
225g/½lb	cod fillet skinned and cooked	½ pound
200g/7oz can	tuna drained	approx. 1 cup
450g/1lb	cooked mashed potato sea salt and freshly ground pepper to taste	1 pound
1 tbs	fresh parsley, chopped rice or wheat flour to coat oil for shallow frying	1 tbs

1. Remove the bones from the cod, and mash together with the tuna.
2. Add the mashed potato and parsley. Season to taste, and mix the ingredients well.
3. Shape into 8 rounds on a floured board and coat with flour.
4. Shallow fry for 5–10 minutes turning once until crisp and golden. Serve with vegetables or salad.

ROLL MOP HERRINGS

Serves 4
Gluten Free   Milk Free   Egg Free

Metric/Imperial		American
4	herrings	4
4 tbs	white vinegar*	4 tbs
140ml/¼ pint	water	⅔ cup
	bay leaf*	
6	peppercorns	6
1 large	onion, cut into rings	1 large

1. Clean, trim and fillet the fish or ask your fishmonger to do it. Wash them well.
2. Roll them up starting from the tail end and pack them closely together in a baking dish.
3. Mix the vinegar and water, pour it over the fish, then add the bay leaf, peppercorns, and onion rings.
4. Bake in the oven, in a covered dish, 350°F/180°C/gas mark 4 for 40 minutes. Serve cold with salad.

HERRINGS IN OATMEAL

Serves 4
Egg Free

Metric/Imperial		American
4	herrings	4
	sea salt and freshly ground pepper	
	oatmeal	
a little	milk	a little
	oil	
	lemon and parsley for garnish	

1. Have the herrings boned, and the heads removed.
2. Add salt and pepper to taste to the oatmeal. Dip the herrings in the milk, then in the oatmeal.
3. Only use a little oil to cook the herrings, as they contain a lot of oil themselves. Cook on both sides until browned.
4. Drain on plain white kitchen paper towels and serve with lemon, parsley and oatcakes (see page 193).

SALMON KEDGEREE

Tuna fish may be used as an alternative to salmon.

Serves 4–5
Gluten Free   Milk Free

Metric/Imperial		American
170g/6oz	brown rice	1 cup
1 tin	salmon	1 can
(approx.		(approx.
200g/7oz)		1 cup)
2 tbs	chopped parsley	2 tbs
3	hard boiled eggs	3
	sea salt and freshly ground	
	pepper to taste if necessary	
	a little oil	

1. Cook rice (see pages 91–2).
2. Mix the rice with the salmon, parsley and two of the hard boiled eggs, chopped. Season if necessary.
3. Heat a little oil in a pan, then add the mixture and heat through.
4. Put on to a warmed serving dish, and arrange the other egg, sliced, on top.

PRAWN SOUFFLÉ

Serves 3–4

Metric/Imperial		American
115g/4oz	peeled prawns	⅔ cup
30g/1oz	margarine or butter	2½ tbs
30g/1oz	85% self-raising flour	¼ cup
½ tsp	mustard powder* (optional)	½ tsp
285ml/½ pint	milk	1⅓ cups
pinch	sea salt and freshly ground pepper	pinch
3	free range eggs, separated	3

1. Lightly oil a 1 litre (2 pint) soufflé dish. Wash prawns.
2. Melt the margarine in a pan. Add flour, mustard powder, milk and salt and pepper to make a sauce. Heat, stirring or whisking continuously until sauce thickens. Add egg yolks and prawns.
3. Beat egg whites until stiff and carefully fold into mixture.
4. Put into soufflé dish and bake at 375°F/190°C/gas mark 5 for 30–35 minutes until well browned. Serve immediately with a green salad.

Note to Cooks

Replace the prawns with any of the following:
1. 115g/4oz/1 cup grated cheese.
2. 115g/4oz/2 cups chopped mushrooms.
3. 170g/6oz/1 cup chopped fish.

BAKED FISH IN YOGURT SAUCE

Serves 4
Egg Free

Metric/Imperial		American
570–680g/ 1¼–1½lb	coley (or other fish of choice)	1¼–1½ pounds
115g/4oz	mushrooms, chopped (optional)	2 cups
3 tbs	oil	3 tbs
2 large	potatoes, sliced	2 large
2 large	carrots, sliced	2 large
	sea salt and freshly ground pepper	
For the sauce:		
30g/1oz	unsalted butter or margarine	2½ tbs
30g/1oz	85% flour	¼ cup
140ml/¼ pint	warm water or stock	⅔ cup
140ml/¼ pint	natural (plain) yogurt	⅔ cup
4 tbs	grated cheddar cheese	4 tbs

1. Wash and skin the fish and place in a greased oven-proof dish.
2. Sauté the mushrooms in a little oil and place over the fish.
3. Peel and slice the potatoes and carrots thinly and sauté in the remaining oil in a large frying pan (skillet) until golden brown, then put around the fish. Season to taste.

Hyperactive Child

To make the sauce:

Melt the butter, blend in the flour and gradually dilute with warm water or vegetable stock. Add the yogurt, and simmer gently for 5 minutes. Pour the sauce over the fish. Cover with grated cheese and bake for 20 minutes in the oven at 375°F/190°C/gas mark 5.

Note to Cooks:

Sour cream can be used for this recipe instead of the yogurt.

FISH PIE

Any cooked flaked white fish, in a little homemade parsley sauce. Add vegetables, and top with mashed potatoes.

4

Meat

LEMON CHICKEN*

Serves 4
Gluten Free   Milk Free   Egg Free

Metric/Imperial		American
1 clove	garlic, skinned and crushed	1 clove
3 tbs	oil	3 tbs
	sea salt and freshly ground pepper to taste	
juice of	2 lemons	juice of
1	onion, skinned and grated	1
8	chicken drumsticks, skinned	8

1. Mix garlic, oil, seasoning, lemon juice and grated onion together in a bowl.
2. Wash and dry chicken pieces. Place them in a shallow dish and pour over the marinade. Leave to marinate for 1–2 hours.

3. Arrange the chicken pieces in the grill (broiler) pan and pour over the marinade. Grill, basting frequently, under medium heat for 30–40 minutes, or until the chicken is cooked through. Serve with any remaining juices.

ROAST LAMB WITH
GARLIC AND ROSEMARY

Gluten Free   Milk Free   Egg Free

1. Use any size or cut of lamb, such as a half leg or shoulder.
2. Crush a garlic clove and rub it over the meat.
3. Insert sprigs of rosemary into the fat of the meat.
4. Roast in a hot oven at 425°F/220°C/gas mark 7 allowing 20 minutes per pound plus 20 minutes, or in a moderate oven at 375°F/190°C/gas mark 5 allowing 30 minutes per pound plus 30 minutes over.
5. Serve with vegetables, saving the cooking water to make the gravy.

GRAVY

Remove the roast from the tin and keep hot. To make thick gravy pour off most of the fat, keeping about a tablespoon and the brown juices. Add a level tablespoon of permitted flour to the juices and stir over a low heat until the flour browns. Add stock or vegetable water, whisk until it nearly boils, then stir until it thickens. Season to taste.

LEMON LAMB MEATBALLS

These are tasty and easy to make.

Serves 4
Egg Free

Metric/Imperial		American
455g/1lb	minced (ground) lamb	1 pound
1	carrot, grated	1
1	potato, washed and grated	1
1 tbs	finely chopped parsley	1 tbs
1 tsp	dried or fresh rosemary*	1 tsp
	sea salt and freshly ground pepper	
55g/2oz	wholemeal (wholewheat) flour or soya (soy) flour	½ cup
140ml/¼ pint	chicken stock	⅔ cup
	finely grated rind of 1 lemon	
2 tbs	lemon juice	2 tbs
2 tbs	natural (plain) yogurt	2 tbs

1. Mix the lamb, carrot, potato, parsley, rosemary, salt and pepper in a bowl.
2. Make into small balls and coat them in the flour. Put in the refrigerator to make firm.
3. Heat a little oil in a frying pan (skillet) and sauté the meatballs until golden brown.
4. Transfer them to a saucepan and add the stock, lemon rind, and juice. Boil gently for ½ hour.

5. When cooked, combine 2 tablespoons of plain yogurt with the pan juices, and pour over.

Notes to Cooks

1. Serve on a bed of brown rice with vegetables of choice.
2. For a gluten free recipe, use only soya (soy) flour.

LAMB AND SWEDE (RUTABAGA) LOAF

This can be eaten hot or cold, with hot vegetables and potato the first day, and with bread and salad the next.

Serves 4
Gluten Free Milk Free

Metric/Imperial		American
1 small	swede (rutabaga)	1 small
2	carrots	2
1 medium-sized	onion	1 medium-sized
455g/1lb	minced (ground) lamb (or beef)	2 cups
1	free range egg, beaten	1
2 tbs	parsley, chopped	2 tbs
1 tbs	soya sauce (wheat-free tamari)	1 tbs
	sea salt and freshly ground pepper to taste	

1. Peel the swede (rutabaga), carrots and onion. Slice and cook in boiling water until soft.
2. While the vegetables are cooking, heat the meat in a large frying pan, stirring all the time, until partially cooked. Drain off any excess fat.
3. Mash together the vegetables, add to the meat with the beaten egg, chopped parsley, soya sauce (wheat-free tamari) and seasoning.

4. Put into a 900g/2-lb loaf tin, pressing down firmly. Bake at 350°F/180°C/gas mark 4 for 45 minutes in the centre of the oven.

Note to Cooks

Suitable for freezing.

SHISH KEBAB

Serves 4
Gluten Free   Milk Free   Egg Free

Metric/Imperial		American
450g/1lb piece	leg of lamb	1 pound piece
	seasoning to taste	
3 tbs	oil	3 tbs
1 tbs	lemon juice	1 tbs
1 clove	garlic, crushed	1 clove
pinch	marjoram*	pinch
1 tbs	chopped parsley	1 tbs
1	onion, sliced	1
	bay leaves (optional)*	

1. Cut the meat into 2cm (1 inch) cubes. Marinate for 2 hours or overnight in the seasoning, oil, lemon juice, garlic, marjoram* and parsley.
2. On four oiled skewers thread the meat cubes, onion slices and bay leaves. Brush with oil and cook under a moderate grill (broiler) for 15–20 minutes, turning about 3 times. If wished you can add button mushrooms or lambs' kidneys. Serve on a bed of plain brown rice with a large green salad.

Note to Cooks

Alternatively, you could use pieces of steak, with slices of onion and mushrooms.

TURKEY BURGERS

Makes 4 medium-sized burgers
Milk Free

Metric/Imperial		American
359g/12oz	minced turkey	1½ cups
1 small	onion, finely chopped or minced	1 small
1	free range egg, beaten sea salt and freshly ground pepper	1
1 tbs	chopped parsley	1 tbs
1 tbs	flour, to bind	1 tbs
1 tbs	oil	1 tbs

1. Mix together all the ingredients except the oil. Shape into four rounds. Dust with flour if necessary.
2. Heat the oil in a frying pan and cook the burgers for about 8 minutes each side, or until cooked right through. Reduce the heat if they are browning too quickly.

LAMB/BEEFBURGERS

Metric/Imperial		American
225g/½lb	minced (ground) lamb or beef	½ pound
1 small	onion, chopped or minced sea salt and freshly ground pepper	1 small
a little	chopped parsley (optional)	a little

1. Mix ingredients together.
2. Shape into flat round cakes and grill or fry. A mould may be used for a more professional finish – a plastic food box lid is ideal. Rinse the lid with cold water, fill with mixture and cover with greaseproof (parchment) paper. Roll firmly with rolling pin and gently ease beefburger out of lid. Burgers can be frozen, interleaved with wax paper.
3. Cook as for Turkey Burgers.

CASSEROLE OF BEEF

Metric/Imperial		American
455g/1lb	stewing steak	1 pound
55g/2oz	wholemeal (wholewheat) flour, seasoned	½ cup
4 sticks	celery or a medium-sized parsnip	4 stalks
2 medium-sized	onions, sliced	2 medium-sized
1 clove	garlic (optional)	1 clove
2 medium-sized	carrots, chopped	2 medium-sized
115g/4oz	mushrooms (optional)	2 cups
2 tbs	oil	2 tbs
1	bay leaf*	1
½ tsp	mixed herbs*	½ tsp
285ml/½ pint	stock	1⅓ cups

1. Cut the beef into small cubes and toss in seasoned flour.
2. Chop all the vegetables.
3. Heat the oil in a pan and sauté the meat in it, at a high heat, until it is browned on all sides. Put on to a separate plate, then sauté the vegetables with the crushed garlic, if used.
4. Put the meat and vegetables into a casserole dish, add the bay leaf and herbs, and pour over the stock.

Meat

5. Cover the casserole and cook in a slow oven 300°F/150°C/gas mark 2 for 2½ hours.
6. Serve with rice or baked potatoes. Will freeze.

TURKEY CASSEROLE

Use the recipe for Casserole of Beef, substituting cubed turkey meat for stewing steak.

COTTAGE PIE BAKE

Serves 4–5
Gluten Free (if rice flour is used)   Egg Free

Metric/Imperial		American
2 tbs	oil	2 tbs
455g/1lb	minced lamb or beef	1 pound
2 medium-sized	onions, finely chopped	2 medium-sized
1 large	carrot, finely chopped	1 large
½ tsp	mixed herbs* (optional)	½ tsp
½ tsp	dried (or 1 tbs fresh) parsley	½ tsp
	sea salt and freshly ground black pepper	
1 tbs	flour	1 tbs
285ml/½ pint	stock	1⅓ cups

For the topping:

455g/1lb	potatoes, mashed	1 pound
455g/1lb	parsnips, mashed	1 pound
55g/2oz	margarine or butter	¼ cup

1. Cook the potatoes and parsnips and mash with the margarine. Preheat the oven to 440°F/200°C/gas mark 6.
2. Heat the oil and sauté the meat for 20 minutes. Drain off any excess fat, then add the onions and carrot. Continue cooking for about 10 minutes until soft. Add the herbs, seasonings and flour and stir in the stock.

Gently heat to simmering point.

3. Turn into a well-greased casserole/baking dish and spread the potato mixture evenly over the top. Bake for about 25 minutes until golden brown.

Note to Cooks

If you prefer, substitute the parsnips with another 455g/1lb of potatoes.

RABBIT CASSEROLE

This recipe often uses cider or wine instead of stock. Non-alcoholic pear juice makes a good substitute, or alternatively you can make stock using 30g (1oz) brown rice miso mixed to a paste with water, or use 1½ tablespoons of natural wheat free soya (soy) sauce (tamari) made up to required amount with water.

Serves 4
Gluten Free   Milk Free   Egg Free

Metric/Imperial		American
455g/1lb	rabbit, cubed	1 pound
2	carrots, sliced (or piece of swede/rutabaga)	2
1	onion, sliced	1
2	leeks, chopped	2
2 sticks	celery, chopped	2 stalks
2 tbs	oil	2 tbs
2 tbs	parsley, chopped	2 tbs
285ml/½ pint	stock or non-alcoholic pear juice	1⅓ cups
	sea salt and freshly ground pepper to taste	

1. Heat oil in a pan and sauté the rabbit cubes at a high heat until browned on all sides. Put on to a separate plate.
2. Sauté the vegetables.

3. Put the meat and vegetables into a casserole dish with the parsley and pour over the stock.
4. Cover the casserole and cook for 1½ hours 350°F/ 180°C/gas mark 4. You can cook it with thin slices of potato on top, and remove the lid of the casserole dish for the last half hour of cooking time, then crisp under the grill.

LIVER LYONNAISE

Serves 4-5
Milk Free Egg Free

Metric/Imperial		American
2 tbs	oil	2 tbs
45g/1½ oz	wholemeal (wholewheat) flour	¼ cup + 1 tbs
285ml/½ pint	stock	1⅓ cups
1	bay leaf*	1
pinch	mixed herbs* and ground black pepper	pinch
2 medium	onions (approx. 225g/ ½ lb [1⅓ cups])	2 medium
2 tbs	white vinegar*	2 tbs
455g/1lb	lambs' liver, sliced seasoned flour for coating	1 pound
1 tbs	oil chopped parsley to garnish	1 tbs

1. To make the sauce, heat 1 tablespoon of oil in a pan, add the flour and allow to brown, then add the stock, bay leaf, herbs and liberal sprinkling of black pepper. Allow the sauce to cook gently for 15 minutes, stirring from time to time and topping up with stock if there is too much evaporation.
2. Slice the onions finely and sauté in 1 tablespoon of oil until golden brown. Drain off excess oil, then add the vinegar and reduce until almost dry. Pass the brown sauce through a sieve on to the onions and allow to

cook together for 5 minutes. The sauce should be of a fairly thin coating consistency.

3. Meanwhile, coat the liver in seasoned flour and sauté quickly in the oil on both sides until cooked.

4. Arrange neatly in a dish, pour over sauce and sprinkle liberally with chopped parsley.

DUMPLINGS

Serves 4
Milk Free   Egg Free

Metric/Imperial		American
115g/4oz	85% self-raising flour	1 cup
55g/2oz	shredded suet	¼ cup
	sea salt and freshly ground pepper to taste	
	water to mix	

1. Add the flour to the suet and seasoning.
2. Mix to a soft dough with the water.
3. Make into balls and add to the casserole for 15–20 minutes, before the end of cooking time.

Notes to Cooks

1. To make parsley dumplings, add a tablespoon of fresh chopped parsley.
2. Vegetarian 'suet' is widely available.

GLUTEN-FREE DUMPLINGS

Serves 4
Gluten Free   Milk Free

Metric/Imperial		American
30g/1oz	margarine (milk free)	2½ tbs
2	free range eggs	2
55g/2oz	rice flour	3 tbs
30g/1oz	potato flour	¼ cup
2 heaped tsp	baking powder (gluten free)	2 heaped tsp
pinch	sea salt and freshly ground pepper	pinch
a little	grated nutmeg* hot stew, soup or broth	a little

1. Soften the margarine and add beaten eggs until creamy. The mixture may curdle but this does not matter.
2. Sieve the flours and baking powder with the nutmeg, salt and pepper. Mix well and gradually add the flours to the eggs and margarine until the mixture forms a stiff paste.
3. Make into 4 dumplings and drop into a simmering stew or soup. Cook for 10–15 minutes and serve.

Note to Cooks

Other flours may be substituted for the above.

YORKIES

Makes 12 small

Metric/Imperial		American
2 tbs	oil	2 tbs
85g/3oz	wholemeal or 85% flour	⅔ cup
1	free range egg, beaten	1
90ml/3 fl oz	milk	⅓ cup
60ml/2 fl oz	water	¼ cup
	sea salt and freshly ground pepper	
30g/1oz	roasted chopped nuts or a mixture of sunflower and sesame seeds	1 oz

1. Preheat the oven to 425°F/220°C/gas mark 7. Divide the oil between a 12-cup bun tray and heat in the hot oven for about 10 minutes until the oil is really hot.
2. To make the batter, sift the flour into a bowl and make a well in the centre. Beat in the egg, and gradually add the milk, water and seasoning, beating until all the ingredients are thoroughly mixed.
3. Add either the toasted chopped nuts or the sunflower and sesame seeds to the batter mixture.
4. Pour about 1 tbs of mixture into each cup of the heated baking tin. Return to the oven for 10–15 minutes until crisp and golden.

5

Pizzas, Flans and Pancakes

HOMEMADE PIZZA

The base is very quick to make but you need longer to cook the vegetables, so prepare them first.

Serves 4

Metric/Imperial		*American*
Topping:		
1 clove	garlic (optional, but nice)	1 clove
340g/¾lb	onions, peeled and chopped	¾ pound
1 tsp	dried mixed herbs*	1 tsp
1 tbs	oil	1 tbs
55–115g/2–4oz	mushrooms	1–2 cups
55g/2oz	grated cheese	½ cup

Crush the garlic. Cook gently with the onions, oil and herbs in a saucepan for about 30–40 minutes, stirring occasionally, until they are a soft mass. While they are cooking prepare the base.

Base:

50g/2oz	margarine	¼ cup
225g/½lb	85% self-raising or organic white flour	2 cups
2	free range eggs water to mix	2

1. Rub the fat into the flour, then add the eggs. Mix to a dough with the water. Roll out thinly and divide into four circles. Place on two greased baking sheets.
2. Spread the prepared onion mixture on top, finely slice the mushrooms and add these, then the grated cheese. Bake for 20–25 minutes at 425°F/220°C/gas mark 7. Will freeze.

Note to Cooks

Alternative toppings:
55g/2oz tin (can) anchovy fillets. Or 125g/4½oz tin (can) sardines in oil. Or add 1 aubergine (eggplant), sliced, to the onions and cook together.

FLANS

Serve with baked potatoes and salad. They are also good for picnics. For gluten-free pastry for the flan case see page 188.

BROCCOLI FLAN

Serves 4

Metric/Imperial		American
1 20cm/8-inch	flan case, baked blind (see page 188) [this takes 170g/6oz (1½ cups) wholemeal or organic white flour and 85g/3oz (⅓ cup) margarine]	1 8-inch
175g/6oz	cottage cheese	½ cup
175g/6oz	broccoli	⅔ cup
2	free range eggs, beaten	2
pinch	mixed herbs*	pinch
pinch	sea salt and freshly ground pepper	pinch

1. Blend or sieve the cottage cheese.
2. Cook the broccoli in a little water until almost soft, then drain and mix well with the other ingredients.
3. Put into prepared flan case and bake in the oven at 375°F/190°C/gas mark 5 for 30–40 minutes until set.

Note to Cooks

For a variation, use 85g/3oz (1½ cups) broccoli and
85g/3oz (approx. ½ cup) carrots (sliced), cooked separately until almost soft.

CHEESE AND CELERY FLAN

Serves 4

Metric/Imperial		*American*
1 23 to 25cm/ 9- to 10-inch	flan case [using 225g/½lb (2 cups) 85% or organic white flour and 115g/4oz (½ cup) fat], baked blind (see page 188)	1 9- to 10-inch
285ml/½ pint	milk	1⅓ cups
3	free range eggs	3
pinch	mixed herbs*	pinch
	sea salt and freshly ground pepper	
115g/4oz	cheese, grated	1 cup
115g/4oz	celery, chopped	1½ cups
1 medium	onion, finely chopped	1 medium
1 tbs	oil	1 tbs

1. Beat together the milk, eggs, herbs, salt and pepper.
2. Arrange most of the grated cheese over the base of the flan.
3. Sauté the celery and onion in a little oil until soft, then drain and add to the flan. Pour over the egg and milk mixture and sprinkle on the remaining cheese.
4. Bake in the oven at 375°F/190°C/gas mark 5 for 30–40 minutes until set and browned on top.

Notes to Cooks

To vary, replace the celery and onion with one of the following:

1. Watercress: one bunch finely chopped.
2. Leeks: 3 medium sized, cut into ½cm (¼ inch) slices, and sauté for approximately 5 minutes.
3. Mushrooms: 115g/4oz (1 cup) and one onion finely chopped. Sauté for approximately 5 minutes.
4. Shrimps or prawns: 115g/4oz (1 cup), added to the milk and egg mixture, with cottage cheese if desired. Will all freeze.

For egg free flans: Substitute a 297g/10½oz pack of silken tofu for the egg and cottage cheese or egg and milk. Whisk or liquidize the tofu until smooth. To give it a yellow colour add ½ teaspoon of turmeric*, and add 1 tablespoon natural soya (soy) sauce for extra flavour.

CAULIFLOWER FRITTERS

Serves 4
Milk Free

Metric/Imperial		American
1 medium-sized	cauliflower	1 medium-sized
	85% or wholemeal flour	
1	free range egg, beaten	1
	wholemeal breadcrumbs	
	for coating	
	oil for frying	

1. Cut the cauliflower into florets and cook for about 8 minutes until just tender. Drain.
2. When cooled a little, dip in seasoned flour, egg and breadcrumbs. Fry in a little oil until crisp. Serve with grated cheese and pasta.

Note to Cooks

You can use other vegetables such as turnips, Jerusalem artichokes or marrow (summer squash) in the same way.

Remember that the dish *will not be milk free* if you serve it with grated cheese.

SAVOURY PANCAKES (CRÊPES)

The pancakes (crêpes) can be made in advance and piled up between sheets of greaseproof paper and kept in the refrigerator or deep freeze. When you want to eat them, fill them with the chosen filling and reheat in the oven at 350°F/180°C/gas mark 4 for 20 minutes.

Makes 10–12

Metric/Imperial		*American*
For the pancakes (crêpes):		
115g/4oz	85% plain or organic white flour	1 cup
pinch	sea salt	pinch
1	free range egg	1
285ml/½ pint	milk and water mixed	1⅓ cups
1 tbs	oil	1 tbs

1. Make a well in the centre of the flour and salt. Add the egg, then the milk and water mixture. Using a wooden spoon, beat well until smooth.
2. Make the pancakes (crêpes) by oiling the pan with a little oil. Use about 2 tablespoons of the batter for each pancake.
3. Cook until base is golden brown, then toss and cook the other side for a short time. Repeat until all the mixture is used.
4. Fill with the desired filling, roll up and serve on a heated dish.

Note to Cooks

For a variation, substitute half of the flour with buck-wheat flour.

Hyperactive Child

88

SAVOURY PANCAKE (CRÊPE) FILLINGS

1. Leeks in Cheese Sauce (see recipe on page 90).
2. Celery, Onion and Beansprout.
   Sauté together 2 sticks (stalks) of celery, 1 medium onion well chopped, and a handful of beansprouts. Add a dash of natural soya (soy) sauce.
3. Beetroot (Beets) and Cottage Cheese.
   455g/1lb (2¾ cups) cooked beetroot (beet), diced, 115g/ 4oz (½ cup) cottage cheese, chopped parsley or chives. Combine, heat gently and fill the pancakes (crêpes).
4. Asparagus.
   Drain a can of asparagus or use cooked fresh asparagus. Add grated cheese and a knob of unsalted butter.
5. Broccoli.
   Cook the broccoli until just soft, add a tablespoon of whipped cream, sea salt, pepper and a dash of lemon juice.

LEEKS IN CHEESE SAUCE

Metric/Imperial		American
30g/1oz	unsalted butter	2½ tbs
30g/1oz	plain 85% flour	¼ cup
285ml/½ pint	milk	1⅓ cups
85g/3oz	cheddar or white cheese, grated	¾ cup
	sea salt and freshly ground pepper	
455g/1lb	cooked leeks	1 pound

1. Make the sauce by melting the butter in the pan, add the flour and milk and whisk until it thickens, then stir and simmer for 5–6 minutes.
2. Stir in the cheese and seasoning. Add the leeks. Divide the filling between the pancakes (crêpes).

6

Rice and Pasta

RICE

Rice has always been a good substitute for potatoes and is tasty with meat, fish, vegetables and salad dishes.

Although brown rice takes a little longer to cook than white rice, it is well worth the effort. It is better nutritionally since it contains some B vitamins and minerals mainly destroyed in the processing of white rice.

Do not be put off by the look of uncooked brown rice as it gets whiter during cooking, and the flavour and texture are much nicer with the added advantage of not having to rinse the starch off.

To Cook Brown Rice

As a guide, use 55g/2oz (¼ cup) of uncooked rice per person.

1. Weigh the dried rice and put into a measuring jug. Make a note of how many fluid ounces (millilitres) it measures in the jug.

2. Double the amount of water or stock to rice.
3. Put the water into a saucepan, bring to the boil and add 1 tbs oil and a pinch of sea salt for every 225g/8oz (1 cup) of rice. Simmer gently for 25–30 minutes or until the rice is soft and all the liquid has been absorbed.

PASTA

Wholemeal Pasta (made from Durum wheat) is again much better than the refined types, for the same reasons as stated for brown rice.

Cook pasta until 'just tender' and in plenty of water – about 1 litre/2 pints (5 cups) to 115g/4oz of pasta. It takes approximately 12 minutes which is roughly 2 minutes longer than the white refined types. 55g/2oz dry weight pasta cooks to one generous portion.

Pasta can be served with all kinds of vegetables, cheese or vegetable sauces, grated cheese, or salads. Even fish or meats can be added in small amounts.

To Cook Lasagne

Cook for approximately 8 minutes in fast-boiling, salted water with a tbs of oil. The sheets should be tender but not soft. Transfer immediately into a bowl of cold water to prevent sheets sticking together. Use as required. The sheets will become soggy if overcooked.

MILLET

Millet is gluten free. Serve as a grain similar to rice. Use in stews, with eggs and savoury dishes. You can also use it to make milk puddings and porridge.

To Cook

1. Wash if necessary, then heat for 2–3 minutes in a saucepan with a little oil.
2. Add boiling water and bring to the boil. For 55g/2oz (¼ cup) of millet, use 570ml/1 pint (2½ cups) of water.
3. Simmer for about 30 minutes until soft and fluffy.

BUCKWHEAT

Buckwheat is also gluten free. It is not really a grain, but comes from plants in the same family as dock leaves. It can be bought roasted or unroasted.

To Cook

1. Use a similar method as for rice. Double the amount of water to the amount of buckwheat.
2. Put the water into a saucepan, bring to the boil and add 1 tbs oil and a pinch of sea salt.
3. Cook for approximately 15 minutes until soft.

Buckwheat Spaghetti might be tried as a change from wholemeal spaghetti or macaroni etc. It cooks well and does not fall to pieces or stick together.

RICE AND CHEESE SAVOURY

Quick and delicious eaten hot or cold.

Serves 4–5
Gluten Free

Metric/Imperial		American
225g/½lb	whole brown rice	1 cup
340g/¾lb	cottage cheese	1½ cups
2	free range eggs	2
2 tbs	yogurt	2 tbs
2 tbs	oil	2 tbs
2 tsp	mixed herbs*	2 tsp
	sea salt and freshly ground pepper	

1. Cook the rice (see pages 91–2).
2. Mix all the ingredients together and put into an oiled ovenproof dish. Cook at 350°F/180°C/gas mark 4 for approximately 30 minutes. Serve hot with vegetables of choice or salad. Will freeze.

Note to Cooks

Add either of the following before mixing together:
1. 1–2 tablespoons chopped parsley.
2. 2 sticks chopped celery (add to the rice 5 minutes before the end of cooking time).

CHINESE RICE

For a gluten free recipe use wheat free soya (soy) sauce (tamari).

Serves 4
Milk Free

Metric/Imperial		American
225g/½lb	brown rice	1 cup
4 tsp	oil	4 tsp
	sea salt and freshly ground pepper	
3	free range eggs, beaten	3
115g/4oz	peeled prawns	¼ pound
115g/4oz	mushrooms, sliced (optional)	1½ cup
115g/4oz	cold cooked chicken, cut into strips	1 cup
4 tbs	chicken stock	4 tbs
1 tbs	natural soya (soy) sauce	1 tbs

1. Cook the rice (see pages 91–2).
2. Heat 1 tsp of oil in a small frying pan. Season beaten eggs and cook to make an omelette. Remove from the pan, cut into strips and keep warm.
3. Heat 2 more teaspoons of oil and lightly fry the prawns. Add the mushrooms (if used) and chicken. Heat through well, then drain and keep hot with the egg strips. Heat the rice gently in the remaining oil, then add stock, soya (soy) sauce and seasoning to

taste. Add all ingredients to the pan and heat through. Put into a hot serving dish and serve immediately, with Stir Fry Vegetables in Sweet & Sour Sauce (see page 97).

STIR FRY VEGETABLES
IN SWEET & SOUR SAUCE

For a gluten free recipe use wheat free soya (soy) sauce
(tamari).

Serves 4
Milk Free   Egg Free

Metric/Imperial		*American*
455g/1lb	mixed vegetables	1 pound
1 tbs	oil	1 tbs
pinch	sea salt	pinch
1 tsp	raw cane sugar	1 tsp
1 tbs	natural soya (soy) sauce	1 tbs
2 pinches	ground ginger*	2 pinches
3 tsp	arrowroot (flour), mixed with 140ml/¼ pint (⅔ cup) vegetable stock	3 tsp

1. Mix your own vegetables, such as bean sprouts, spring onions (scallions), celery, broccoli, cauliflower, carrots, turnips, mushrooms or cabbage. Cut them into very thin slices, or small diagonal chunks or matchsticks.
2. Heat the oil in a pan or wok. Add the 'hard' vegetables first and fry at a high heat for a minute, then add the soft vegetables and fry for 2 minutes.
3. Add the salt, sugar, soya (soy) sauce, ginger and arrowroot mixture. Mix well and cook until the sauce thickens. Serve hot with Chinese Rice (see page 95).

PASTA NESTS

Serves 4
Milk Free   Egg Free

Metric/Imperial		American
340g/¾lb	chicken, small diced/ bite sized	¾ pound
1 tbs	light soya (soy) sauce	1 tbs
2 tbs	wholemeal or 85% flour	2 tbs
2 tbs	oil	2 tbs
340g/¾lb	tagliatelle	¾ pound
4 medium-sized	carrots, thinly sliced or cut into strips	4 medium-sized
4 sticks	celery, thinly sliced	4 stalks
100g/4oz	mushrooms, sliced (optional)	1 cup
4 tbs	pineapple juice	4 tbs

1. Coat the chicken with the soya (soy) sauce and flour. Heat the oil in a large frying pan or wok and stir fry for about 10–15 minutes until cooked. Put to one side.
2. Cook the pasta according to the directions on the packet (or see page 93).
3. While the pasta is cooking, stir fry the vegetables in a little oil for approximately 5–8 minutes, depending on how crisp you like your vegetables. Add the pineapple juice, then the chicken, and stir together well.
4. Drain the pasta and arrange in a ring on each of 4 warmed plates. Fill the nests with the chicken mixture and serve immediately.

PASTA SALAD

Serves 4–6
Milk Free   Egg Free

Metric/Imperial		American
170g/6oz	pasta shapes	2 cups
115g/4oz	broccoli florets	2 cups
2	carrots, grated	2
1 200g/7-oz tin	pineapple chunks in own juice	1 200g/ 7-oz can
170g/6oz	bean sprouts	1 cup

Dressing

4 tbs	pineapple juice	4 tbs
1 tbs	soya (soy) sauce	1 tbs
6 tbs	sunflower oil	6 tbs

1. Cook the pasta according to directions on the packet (or see page 93). Drain well. Cook the broccoli florets in boiling water for about 3 minutes, then drain.
2. In a large bowl, mix together the pasta, carrots, pineapple and bean sprouts.
3. In a small bowl, beat together all the dressing ingredients and add to the pasta with the broccoli. Toss to coat. Cool and serve.

Note to Cooks

For variation, use a tin of tuna in place of bean sprouts, or ½ tsp sesame oil in place of all sunflower oil.

CHICKEN LASAGNE

Serves 4
Egg Free

Metric/Imperial		American
350g/12oz	chicken, boned and skinned	12oz
115g/4oz	mushrooms, sliced	½ cup
1 medium-sized	onion, chopped	1 medium-sized
1	clove garlic, chopped (optional)	1
1 tsp	dried basil	1 tsp
140ml/¼ pint	chicken stock	⅔ cup
2 tbs	oil	2 tbs
2 tbs	wholemeal or 85% flour	2 tbs
285ml/½ pint	milk	1⅓ cups
	sea salt and freshly ground pepper to taste	
170g/6oz	lasagne	6oz
850ml/1½ pints	water	3¾ cups
55g/2oz	cheese, grated	½ cup

1. Cook the chicken in a covered dish in the oven or microwave. Keep the meat juices for stock and chop the chicken into small pieces.
2. Put the mushrooms, onion, garlic and basil into a saucepan with the stock. Bring to the boil and cook for 10 minutes or until soft. Drain, but reserve the liquid.
3. Heat the oil in a saucepan, stir in the flour and cook gently for 1 minute. Gradually add the milk, bring to

the boil and simmer for 3 minutes, stirring all the time as the sauce thickens. Use the reserved vegetable liquid to thin the stock as required. Add salt and pepper to taste. Mix in the chicken and vegetables.

4. Cook the lasagne in fast-boiling, salted water with a tbs of oil until tender but not soft (see page 93).

5. Lightly oil an ovenproof dish and layer the lasagne and chicken mixture alternately in the dish, starting with the chicken mixture and ending with the pasta. Pour over the remaining sauce and sprinkle with grated cheese.

6. Bake at 375°F/190°C/gas mark 5 for approximately 25–30 minutes.

LIVER GOUJONS WITH PASTA

Serves 4
Milk Free

Metric/Imperial		American
340g/12oz	lamb's liver	12oz
5 tbs	wholemeal flour	5 tbs
	sea salt and freshly ground	
	black pepper	
1	free range egg, beaten	1
115g/4oz	fine oatmeal	½ cup
3 tbs	oil	3 tbs
1 medium-sized	onion, finely sliced	1 medium-sized
285ml/½ pint	stock (use additive-free stock cube)	1⅓ cups
2 tbs	lemon juice and rind of 1 lemon	2 tbs
1 tsp	dried (or 2 tbs fresh) parsley, chopped	1 tsp
340g/12oz	tagliatelle	12oz

1. Cut the liver into strips (5cm/2-in by 1¼cm/½-in) and coat with 3 tbs of seasoned flour.
2. Dip the liver strips into the beaten egg, then into the oatmeal. Keep in the fridge while preparing the sauce.
3. Beat 1 tbs of oil in a saucepan, add the onion and cook gently until lightly browned. Add the remaining flour, then gradually add the stock, lemon juice, rind,

parsley and seasoning. Bring to the boil, stirring all the time, then simmer gently for 10–15 minutes.

4. While the sauce is cooking, put the tagliatelle into a large saucepan of boiling, salted water. Add 1 tbs of oil. Return to the boil, then reduce heat and cook for 12 minutes or until tender.

5. Heat the remaining oil in a large frying pan, then add the liver goujons. Cook for 2–4 minutes, turning frequently until tender and cooked.

6. Drain the pasta well and put into a warmed serving dish. Pour over the sauce, and arrange the liver on top. Garnish with parsley, and serve with a green salad.

7

Pulses and Beans

T O PREPARE pulses, check for broken or damaged ones as well as any grit. Wash well. All beans need soaking except lentils, mung beans, aduki beans and black eye beans. These will cook in 20–40 minutes.

Soak all other pulses overnight in cold water or in boiling water for 2 hours. Always cover with plenty of water as pulses swell to more than twice their size. The beans are now ready to cook.

All beans need to be thoroughly cooked or they will be very indigestible and could make you ill.

Put beans in a saucepan and cover with clean fresh water. Bring to the boil, skim and boil at over 100°C for 10 minutes to destroy toxins. Make sure you boil the beans for 10 minutes even if you use a pressure cooker. Do not add salt in cooking as beans and peas may not soften at all. Add a bay leaf instead or herbs and spices of choice. Add salt when cooked if required.

It is always best to cook pulses first before adding to casseroles, savoury dishes, etc. otherwise vegetables can become overcooked.

There are endless combinations you can try for yourself. Cook more than required of each variety and freeze in small amounts for adding to salads or casseroles.

COOKING TIMES FOR BEANS

All beans must be cooked until soft and must be seen to boil hard for a minimum of 10 minutes.

Aduki Beans	30–40 mins. (No need to soak)
Black Eye Beans	30–40 mins. (No need to soak)
Butter Beans (Lima Beans)	1–1½ hrs.
Canellini Beans	1 hr.
Chickpeas (Garbanzo Beans)	4 hrs.
Flageolet Beans	1 hr.
Haricot Beans (Navy Beans)	1½ hrs.
Kidney Beans	1–2 hrs.
Lentils	30 mins. (No need to soak)
Mung Beans	30–40 mins. (No need to soak)
Borlotti Beans (Pinto Beans)	1–1¼ hrs.
Soya Beans (Soy Beans)	3–4 hrs.

SPECIAL SAVOURY LENTILS

This is one of those dishes which actually improves with re-heating so you can prepare it in advance. It's very filling and delicious, just serve it with hunks of wholemeal (wholewheat) bread.

Grain Free   Gluten Free   Milk Free   Egg Free

Metric/Imperial		American
225g/½lb	brown lentils	1 cup
570–710ml 1–1¼ pints	vegetable stock (or use allowed stock cube)	2½–3 cups
1	bay leaf*	1
1 tsp	mixed herbs*	1 tsp
1 large	onion	1 large
1–2 or more	cloves garlic, crushed	1–2 or more
1	carrot, grated	1
225g/½lb	mixed vegetables, such as swede (rutabaga), turnip, parsnip, celery, white cabbage or mushrooms sea salt and freshly ground pepper	½ pound
1–2 tbs	oil	1–2 tbs
1–2 tbs	lemon juice or to taste	1–2 tbs

1. Wash the lentils, look for damaged ones, and check there is no grit. Cook for about 15 minutes in the stock with the bay leaf and mixed herbs.

2. While the lentils are cooking prepare and dice the vegetables.
3. Heat the oil in a pan and sauté the vegetables for a few minutes. Add them to the lentils and simmer altogether for another 15 to 20 minutes, adding more stock if it seems too dry. Season to taste.
4. When the lentils and vegetables are soft remove the bay leaf.
5. Just before serving, add the lemon juice to taste.

LENTIL ROAST

Serves 4–5
Gluten Free

Metric/Imperial		American
225g/½lb	lentils, whole or split	1 cup
425ml/¾ pint	water or vegetable stock	2 cups
1	bay leaf*	1
1 tbs	oil	1 tbs
1 medium	onion, chopped	1 medium
1 clove	garlic, crushed (optional)	1 clove
2 sticks	celery, chopped finely	2 stalks
1 tsp	mixed herbs* or 2 tbs chopped parsley	1 tsp
115g/4oz	cheddar cheese, grated	1 cup
1 tbs	lemon juice	1 tbs
1	free range egg, beaten sea salt and freshly ground pepper to taste	1

1. Wash the lentils and check there is no grit. Simmer in the water or stock with the bay leaf for 20–30 minutes (12–15 minutes for split lentils) until all the moisture has been absorbed.
2. Heat the oil in a pan and sauté the chopped onion, garlic and celery until soft but not brown.
3. Put the other ingredients into a mixing bowl, and add the sautéed vegetables to them, then mix together with the lentils. Season to taste.

Hyperactive Child

4. Turn the mixture on to a floured board and form into a roll shape, coating well with flour. Place on to a greased pie dish or baking sheet and bake for 45 minutes until crisp at 375°F/190°C/gas mark 5. Will freeze.

BAKED BEANS

For a gluten-free recipe, omit mustard powder.

Serves 3–4
Milk Free   Egg Free

Metric/Imperial		American
1	onion, finely chopped	1
1 tbs	oil	1 tbs
30g/1oz	rice flour	2 tbs
½ tsp	mustard powder*	½ tsp
285ml/½ pint	water or bean stock	1½ cups
1 tbs	lemon juice	1 tbs
1 tbs	black treacle or molasses*	1 tbs
1 tsp	raw cane sugar	1 tsp
pinch	sea salt	pinch
225g/½lb	haricot (navy) or soya (soy) beans, cooked	1 cup

1. Sauté chopped onion in the oil for a few minutes until soft. Mix flour and mustard powder to a smooth sauce with a little of the cold water. Add to onion with all other ingredients.
2. Mix well and simmer gently for approximately 20 minutes. Will freeze.

Note to Cooks

Replace rice flour with flours to suit your requirements.

8

Vegetables and Cheese

VEGETABLE MEDLEY

Leeks are used in this recipe, but you can use any
vegetable you like, such as marrow, carrots, celery, broccoli, Jerusalem artichokes or cauliflower. Allow about
1 lb of prepared vegetables and follow the method below.

Serves 4

Metric/Imperial		American
455g/1lb	leeks	1 pound
30g/1oz	unsalted butter	1oz
30g/1oz	85% flour	1oz
425ml/¾ pint	milk	2 cups
2 tbs	lemon juice	2 tbs
rind of ½	lemon (optional)	rind of ½
	sea salt and freshly ground black pepper	
115g/4oz	breadcrumbs	2 cups
4	hardboiled free range eggs	4
1–2 tbs	chopped parsley	1–2 tbs

1. Remove roots from the leeks, cut down one side and clean carefully. Cut off the green parts and chop into ½cm (¼-inch) slices. Cook in a little boiling water until tender, and drain well.
2. Make the sauce by melting the butter in a saucepan, then adding the flour and milk. Whisk together and gently heat until the sauce begins to thicken, then stir to make a smooth sauce. Gradually add the lemon juice and seasoning, and simmer gently for 5–6 minutes.
3. To prepare the topping, toast the breadcrumbs under the grill, turning frequently until crisp and golden brown. Finely chop the hardboiled eggs and add to the breadcrumbs with the parsley and lemon rind, and salt and pepper to taste.
4. Put the leeks on a warm serving dish. Pour over the sauce and top with the breadcrumb mixture. Garnish with lemon slices and parsley.

VEGETABLE PIE

This makes a delicious meal, and you can vary the vegetables according to the season. For a milk-free recipe, omit the yogurt and lemon juice and add 140ml/¼ pint (⅔ cup) of stock instead.

Serves 4
Egg Free

Metric/Imperial		American
455g/1lb	prepared vegetables (such as 1 medium onion, 1 turnip, diced small, 1 carrot, diced small, ¼ cabbage, ¼ cauliflower)	1 pound
1 tbs	oil	1 tbs
1 tbs	lemon juice	1 tbs
285ml/½ pint	natural (plain) yogurt	1⅓ cups

1. Chop the vegetables then fry gently in the oil until soft (about 10 minutes).
2. Mix together the vegetables, lemon juice and yogurt and put into a lightly oiled pie dish.

To make the potato and cheese pie crust:

55g/2oz	potatoes, mashed	⅓ cup
30g/1oz	butter or margarine	1 oz
55g/2oz	cheese, grated	½ cup
55g/2oz	oatmeal	⅓ cup

Vegetables and Cheese

115g/4oz	flour	1 cup
pinch	sea salt	pinch
	water to mix	

1. Mash the potatoes with the butter or margarine. Mix together the cheese, oatmeal, flour and salt and stir into the potato. Mix to a stiff dough with the water.
2. Roll out the dough on a floured board and cover the vegetables. Trim the edges and bake at 400°F/200°C/gas mark 6 for approximately 1 hour until golden brown.

Note to Cooks

Suitable for freezing.

VEGETABLE CRUMBLE

Prepare and cook the vegetables as for Vegetable Pie but substitute the crumble for the pie crust.

Serves 4
Gluten Free   Egg Free

Metric/Imperial		American
55g/2oz	soft margarine	¼ cup
140g/5oz	85% flour	1 cup
30g/1oz	ground hazelnuts	⅓ cup
30g/1oz	sesame seeds	¼ cup
1 tsp	mixed herbs*	1 tsp
	or 2 tbs fresh parsley	
	sea salt and freshly	
	ground black pepper	

1. Rub the fat into the flour, or mix with a fork. Add the nuts, seeds, herbs, salt and pepper. Put the crumble over the vegetables and bake as for Vegetable Pie.

CARROT AND POTATO LOAF

Serves 3–4

Gluten Free   Milk Free

Metric/Imperial		American
170g/6oz	raw grated carrot	1 cup
170g/6oz	celery, grated	1 cup
85g/3oz	soft margarine (milk free)	⅓ cup
115g/4oz	soya (soy) flour	1 cup
280g/10oz	cooked mashed potato	1¼ cups
2	free range eggs, lightly beaten	2
pinch	sea salt and freshly ground black pepper	pinch
½ tsp	celery salt	½ tsp

1. Mix the carrots, celery, margarine, flour and potato well together.
2. Pour beaten eggs over the mixture and add seasoning. Mix well.
3. Turn into an oiled 450g/1lb loaf tin and bake in oven at 325°F/170°C/gas mark 3 for approximately 1 hour and 15 minutes until set.

Notes to Cooks

Serve with greens or leaf salad. Good hot or cold. Suitable for freezing.

CELEBRATION NUT ROAST

This is a wonderful nut roast, good enough for Christmas dinner for vegetarians. Eat it hot or cold with potatoes and salad. It is also tasty in sandwiches.

Serves 4
Milk Free

Metric/Imperial		American
3 tbs	wholemeal (wholewheat) breadcrumbs	3 tbs
170g/6oz	mixed nuts, eg:	1½ cups
55g/2oz	cashews or brazils	½ cup
55g/2oz	sunflower seeds	½ cup
55g/2oz	hazelnuts or (English) walnuts	½ cup
2	carrots, grated	2
1 large	onion	1 large
4 sticks	celery	4 stalks
4 tbs	parsley, chopped	4 tbs
30g/1oz	ground sesame seeds	3 tbs
½ tsp	ground cumin*	½ tsp
½ tsp	celery salt	½ tsp
2	free range eggs	2
	sea salt and freshly ground pepper	

1. Grind the breadcrumbs and nuts until fine. Mix together with the grated carrot, chopped onion and celery.

2. Add the remaining ingredients, mixing well.
3. Press into an oiled 455g/1lb baking tin and bake for 1 hour at 400°F/200°C/gas mark 6. Will freeze.

BRUSSELS SPROUTS WITH CHESTNUTS

Serves 4
Gluten Free   Egg Free

Metric/Imperial		American
455g/1lb	Brussels sprouts	1 pound
15g/½oz	unsalted butter or margarine	1 tbs
115g/¼ lb	peeled chestnuts	¾ cup
	sea salt and freshly ground pepper	

1. Cook the sprouts until just tender, drain, and toss in the butter.
2. Meanwhile, cook the chestnuts in boiling water with a pinch of salt until tender but not broken.
3. Add chestnuts and seasoning to the sprouts. Serve very hot, with any main meal.

WATERCRESS CHEESY PUDDING

Serves 4

This makes a nourishing, tasty supper or high tea and looks quite pretty when cooked.

Metric/Imperial		*American*
1 bunch	watercress	1 bunch
425ml/¾ pint	milk	2 cups
30g/1oz	butter or margarine	2½ tbs
115g/4oz	wholemeal (wholewheat) breadcrumbs	2 cups
115g/4oz	cheddar cheese, grated sea salt and freshly ground pepper	1 cup
1 tsp	made (prepared) mustard*	1 tsp
2	free range eggs, separated	2

1. Wash the watercress well, then chop finely.
2. Heat the milk and butter in a pan until the butter has melted, remove from the heat and mix in the breadcrumbs, cheese and seasoning. Add the mustard, egg yolks and chopped watercress.
3. Whisk the egg whites until stiff and fold lightly into the pudding.
4. Put into an oiled pie dish and bake in oven for about 20 minutes at 400°F/200°C/gas mark 6, until set and lightly brown on top. Will freeze.
5. Serve with salad or cooked vegetables. Swede and carrots look attractive.

Hyperactive Child

BREAD AND BUTTER CHEESE PUDDING

Serves 3–4

Metric/Imperial		*American*
4 slices	bread and butter	4 slices
85g/3oz	cheese, grated	¾ cup
2	free range eggs	2
	sea salt and freshly ground pepper	
1 tbs	fresh (or 1 tsp dried) parsley	1 tbs
425ml/¾ pint	milk	2 cups

1. Oil an ovenproof pie dish. Cut each slice of bread and butter into four. Arrange a layer of bread over the base of the dish so that the slices overlap. Sprinkle with grated cheese and continue to make alternate layers of bread and cheese.
2. Beat the eggs and add the seasoning. Gradually add the milk, whisking thoroughly. Pour slowly over the bread and cheese mixture and leave to soak for 10 minutes.
3. Bake at 350°F/180°C/gas mark 4 for 30–35 minutes until golden brown.

POTATOES SESAME STYLE

The sesame seeds are an excellent source of calcium, especially for anyone on a milk-free diet. A satisfying meal if served with the cheese, it can also accompany a main meal.

Serves 4

Gluten Free   Egg Free   Milk Free (if not using cheese)

Metric/Imperial		American
4	baking potatoes	4
a little	oil	a little
2 tbs	sesame seeds	2 tbs
115g/4oz	cheese (optional)	1 cup

1. Pre-heat oven to 400°F/200°C/gas mark 6.
2. Scrub the potatoes and cut parallel slices almost down to the base. Brush with oil and roll the top firmly into the sesame seeds.
3. Bake for about 1 hour, until tender inside and crispy brown outside. Serve with a main meal.
4. If using the cheese, cut small slices to fit inside the opened-out potato slices. Return to the oven for a few minutes until the cheese melts.

POTATO AND CHEESE MOULD

This recipe is tasty and well worth trying.

Serves 4

Metric/Imperial		American
	toasted breadcrumbs	
340g/¾lb	mashed potatoes	1½ cups
14g/½oz	margarine or butter	1¼ tbs
2 tbs	milk	2 tbs
	sea salt and freshly	
	ground black pepper	
55g/2oz	grated cheese	½ cup
2	free range eggs, separated	2

1. Grease a 1-litre/2-pint (5-cup) pudding basin with butter or margarine and coat with the breadcrumbs.
2. Mash the potatoes with the margarine, 1 tbs of the milk and add salt and pepper to taste. Put through a sieve. Add the grated cheese, egg yolks and the rest of the milk. Mix well.
3. Whisk the egg whites until stiff and stir gently into the mixture. Put into the basin which should be three parts full.
4. Bake at 350°F/180°C/gas mark 4 for 50 minutes until firm and slightly brown on top. Loosen edges with a palette knife and turn out onto a hot serving dish. Garnish with a little parsley or watercress.

Note to Cooks

Good eaten with salad or vegetables. Serve hot or cold. Cuts into small wedges ideal for picnics and parties.

CHEESY SAUSAGES

These are delicious. Serve them with jacket potatoes and salad.

Makes 8

Metric/Imperial		*American*
115g/4oz	cheddar cheese, grated	1 cup
115g/4oz	wholemeal breadcrumbs	2 cups
2 tbs	chopped parsley	2 tbs
1 tbs	chopped chives or spring onion tops (optional)	1 tbs
1 tsp	mustard powder*	1 tsp
½ tsp	sea salt and freshly ground black pepper	½ tsp
1	free range egg yolk	1
a little	water to mix	a little
1 tbs	oil	1 tbs

Coating:

1	free range egg white	1
55g/2oz	wholemeal breadcrumbs	1 cup

1. Mix together the cheese, breadcrumbs, parsley, chives, mustard, salt and pepper.
2. Add the egg yolk and stir in a little water to bind the mixture into a ball.
3. Roll into 8 sausage shapes, dip them into the egg white, then the remaining breadcrumbs.

4. Heat the oil and cook the sausages over a moderate heat, taking care not to burn them. Turn frequently to brown them evenly.

LEFTOVER IDEAS

SCRAMBLED EGG WITH VEGETABLES

Add any cooked vegetables of choice – runner beans, beansprouts and mushrooms, etc. to egg mixture and cook as usual. Serve on bread and butter, toast and/or with salad greens, e.g. lettuce, watercress.

BUBBLE AND SQUEAK

1. Chop cooked leftover sprouts or cabbage and mix with mashed potato. Season to taste. Fry in a little oil until brown.
2. Serve with scrambled or poached egg.

9

Salads

FRESH SALADS are full of vitamins and minerals and contain fibre and moisture which aids thirst. They need to be chewed well, like all unrefined foods, and this helps to keep the teeth and jaws healthy. Try to have some raw salad daily, as this is better than an occasional large one. If you are not used to eating raw salad foods, gradually build up to a meal by adding one raw item grated in small amounts (1 tsp) with other foods. It is important for everyone, especially children, to obtain adequate vitamin C. If the children cannot eat the fruits containing salicylates they can still get plenty of vitamin C from fresh raw vegetables and grapefruit, lemons, limes etc. Parsley is also rich in vitamin C.

A daily salad could contain any of the following, but always include a leafy green.

Grated raw or cooked carrots, grated raw cauliflower, grated raw celeriac, grated raw turnip, grated raw celery, chives, Chinese leaves (keeps longer than lettuce), cress, endive, fennel (slice finely or chop), garlic, lettuce, onion, parsley, cabbage (red or white, shredded), spring onions (scallions), Brussels sprouts (shredded), sprouted beans and seeds (beansprouts), watercress, young tender spinach leaves (lovely raw in place of lettuce).

DRESSINGS

These help improve the flavour, food value and digestibility. Vinegar or lemon juice helps to preserve the vitamin C. The oil helps to absorb the fat soluble vitamins, such as vitamin A in carrots.

BEANSPROUTS

These are very cheap and easy to grow. Children love to watch things grow, and it makes it especially exciting if they can eat and enjoy what they have grown themselves. Beansprouts are nutritious, containing vitamins, minerals and fibre.

Put 1 tablespoon (level) of chosen beans or seeds in a clean jam jar and cover the top of the jar with muslin or similar material, to allow for water to filter through. Secure with a rubber band.

Keep away from direct heat or sunlight.

Fill the jar with warm water and drain. Repeat 2 or 3 times a day. The seeds will grow from around the sides of the jar. The original volume will increase about 8–10 times before they are ready to eat, in 3 to 6 days.

Discontinue growing after 6 days as flavour will be lost. Discard any seeds that have not sprouted for two to three days. Sprouts will keep in the fridge.

Salads

They can also be grown in a dark cupboard on blotting paper in a plastic container.

Eat sprouts raw in salads, sandwiches, etc., or add a few (1–2 cups) to casseroles, soups, etc., about 15 minutes before cooking time is up.

Note: Only eat raw sprouted beans and not their seeds as these are likely to make you ill. Most beans can be sprouted except red or white kidney beans.

The most popular are:- Mung beans, alfalfa seeds, aduki beans, green lentils, whole (uncracked) wheat grain.

FENNEL

The seeds can be used to make tea. They can be cooked with cabbage, or sprinkled on bread rolls or cereals. The feathery leaves can be used in a sauce for fish dishes or chicken. The bulbous root can be thinly sliced and combined with a French Dressing and added to a green salad. They have a delicious aniseed flavour. To cook, boil in water until tender.

AVOCADO PEARS

Although these are not always to children's taste, they do contain a good supply of vitamins and minerals, and more protein than any other fruit. They also contain saturated and polyunsaturated fat. You can add cubed avocado to salads, tossing the cubes first in oil and vinegar, or lemon juice. Or you can halve the avocado, removing the stone and filling the cavity with prawns (shrimps), or cottage cheese, brushing the surface first with lemon juice to stop discolouration. Let the children plant the stone to grow their own plant.

SWEET POTATOES

Baked

Scrub and oil the skins. Bake small ones whole or cut large ones into even slices. Cook until tender, 40 to 60 minutes. Serve with butter or margarine.

Boiled

Can be boiled in their skins for 20–30 minutes. Then peel, slice, dot with butter or margarine and season with sea salt and freshly ground pepper.

Mashed

Cook as for boiled sweet potato, and mash with a little hot milk, butter or margarine and sea salt.

GLOBE ARTICHOKES

These are delicious served hot with butter or Hollandaise sauce, or cold with a salad dressing, such as mayonnaise flavoured with chopped herbs, prawns, shrimps or mashed tuna fish. You can also use sour cream. First wash the artichoke and cut off the stem, then upper leaves. Boil for 45 minutes in salted water with a squeeze

Salads

of lemon juice, or 7 to 10 minutes in a pressure cooker. Drain and cool, then twist the inner cone of leaves, take out and throw away. Scrape out all the hairy choke with a spoon and discard. Fill the centre with the dressing of your choice. Pull off the leaves, dipping them into the dressing, then eat the soft parts. When the leaves are gone, eat the heart which is delicious.

FUN SALADS

Make faces on a plate. Here are some suggestions, and no doubt you will find many more.

Put a large lettuce leaf on a plate and add the following as required:-

To Make Eyes

Carrot – small piles raw and grated.
Mushroom – thinly sliced.
Egg – sliced hard boiled.

To Make a Nose

Celery stick.
Quiche/Flan – small slice (hot or cold).
Additive-free savoury sausage – (hot or cold).
Brown rice or pasta – make a long thin pile (hot).
Beans (pulses) – make a long thin pile (hot).
Meat – cut into strips (hot or cold).
Fish – for example, sardine.

To Make Cheeks

Make 2 heaps of any of the following:
Carrot – raw and grated.
Lettuce heart.
Chinese leaves – shredded.
Cottage cheese or grated hard cheese.

To Make a Mouth

Lettuce – or most of the above.
Additive-free savoury sausage (hot or cold).
Sardine.
Scrambled egg – (hot or cold).
Cheese.

To Make Hair

Watercress.
Sprouting beans.
Mustard and cress.
Nuts or seeds.

BANANA SALAD

Gluten Free

1. Arrange some mustard and cress, watercress or lettuce on plates. Cut 2 or 3 large bananas in half then in 4 lengthways. Brush with lemon juice.
2. Arrange banana as spokes in a wheel. Put slices of hard boiled egg or small heaps of chopped nuts, figs and/or cottage cheese around plate.

RICE SALAD

Serves 4
Gluten Free   Milk Free   Egg Free

Metric/Imperial		American
225g/½ lb	brown rice	1 cup
2	spring onions (scallions), finely chopped	2
1 small clove	garlic, crushed (optional)	1 small clove
2 sticks	celery, finely chopped	2 stalks
1	carrot, finely chopped	1
6	black olives, stoned* (optional)	6
3 tbs	safflower, sunflower or olive oil	3 tbs
1 tbs	lemon juice	1 tbs
1 tsp	basil*	1 tsp
	sea salt and freshly ground pepper	

1. Boil the rice until tender, but still firm. While the rice is still warm add the remaining ingredients and season to taste.

Note to Cooks

A recipe for Pasta Salad can be found on page 99.

BEAN SALAD

Metric/Imperial		American
225g/½lb	cooked beans, either red kidney beans or a mixture of red, white and green flageolets (cook separately to preserve the colours)	1 cup
1 tbs	sunflower or olive oil	1 tbs
1 tsp	lemon juice	1 tsp
	sea salt and freshly ground pepper to taste	
1 tbs	chopped parsley	1 tbs
1 clove	garlic (optional)	1 clove

1. Rub a bowl with the garlic clove (if used).
2. Mix all the other ingredients well together while the beans are still warm. Chill in the fridge before serving.

Note to Cooks

You can soak and cook larger quantities of beans, then freeze them, and bring out smaller quantities when you fancy a salad. If you mix the beans they look very pretty glistening in the dressing.

CARROT SALAD

Serves 3–4
Gluten Free   Milk Free   Egg Free

Metric/Imperial		American
1	pear, cut into small pieces	1
	lemon juice (a squeeze)	
2–3	carrots, grated	2–3
55g/2oz	chopped (English) walnuts	½ cup
1 punnet	mustard and cress	1 punnet

1. Sprinkle lemon juice over chopped pears and grated carrot to prevent discolouration.
2. Mix and enjoy.

BEANSPROUT AND CASHEW NUT SALAD

Serves 3–4
Gluten Free   Milk Free   Egg Free

Metric/Imperial		American
115g/4oz	beansprouts	2 cups
2 sticks	celery, chopped finely	2 stalks
2	carrots, grated	2
55g/2oz	cashew nuts	½ cup

Dressing:

1 tsp	clear honey*	1 tsp
2 tsp	safflower or sunflower oil	2 tsp
2 tsp	lemon juice	2 tsp

1. Mix the beansprouts with the celery, grated carrots and cashew nuts.
2. Mix the dressing ingredients and pour over the salad.

GREEN SALAD

Serves 4
Gluten Free   Milk Free   Egg Free

Metric/Imperial		American
1	lettuce or half Chinese leaves	1
1 carton	cress	1 carton
1 tbs	chopped parsley	1 tbs
1 clove	garlic (optional)	1 clove
2 tbs	French Dressing (see page 145)	2 tbs

1. Wash the vegetables, and mix together.
2. Rub a bowl with the garlic clove (if used), and add the vegetables. Mix the dressing and season to taste. Pour onto the vegetables and toss to mix.

MELON AND PRAWN SALAD

Serves 4
Gluten Free   Milk Free

Metric/Imperial		American
1	melon, cubed	1
170g/6oz	peeled prawns	1⅓ cups
285ml/½ pint	mayonnaise (additive free)	1⅓ cups
1 tsp	grated lemon rind	1 tsp
	watercress or lettuce	
	whole prawns and	
	watercress to garnish	

1. Mix the melon with the prawns.
2. Add the mayonnaise, and the lemon rind and stir until the melon and prawns are coated.
3. Arrange on a bed of lettuce or watercress. Garnish with whole prawns and watercress.
4. Serve with wholemeal bread or rolls and butter.

MELON, GINGER AND CURD CHEESE SALAD

Serves 4
Gluten Free   Egg Free

Metric/Imperial		American
1 large	ripe honeydew melon	1 large
170g/6oz	curd (pot) cheese or Quark	¾ cup
1 level tsp	ground ginger* (optional)	1 level tsp
1 clove	garlic, skinned and crushed	1 clove
	sea salt and freshly	
	ground pepper to taste	
	parsley to garnish	

1. Cut the melon lengthways into four. Scoop out the seeds.
2. Put the cheese in a bowl and work in the ginger, garlic and seasoning.
3. Pile into the centres of the melon pieces and garnish with parsley.

CAULIFLOWER SALAD

Serves 4
Gluten Free   Milk Free

Metric/Imperial		American
340g/¾lb	prepared cauliflower	2 cups
1	firm pear, chopped and cored	1
2	hardboiled eggs, chopped	2
70ml/⅛ pint	mayonnaise or salad cream (additive free)	⅓ cup
2–3 tsp	lemon juice freshly ground sea salt and pepper to taste	2–3 tsp

1. Break the cauliflower into small florets and wash well. If preferred, cook for 2–3 minutes in boiling water. Florets should still be crunchy. Allow to cool.
2. Put all ingredients into a salad bowl, season if wished, and toss well together.

COLESLAW

Makes 455g/1lb (1 pound)
Gluten Free   Milk Free

Metric/Imperial		American
225g/8oz	white cabbage	2 cups
115g/4oz	celery, chopped	1 cup
1 small	onion, grated (optional)	1 small
55g/2oz	carrots, grated	½ cup
	mayonnaise (additive free)	
	to coat	

1. Shred the cabbage very finely.
2. Add the chopped celery, onion and grated carrot.
3. Mix all the ingredients together with the mayonnaise.

Note to Cooks

You can add 55g/2oz (½ cup) chopped cashew nuts or dates for variety.

HOMEMADE SALAD CREAM

Children often seem to prefer this to the real mayonnaise. You will find it will keep for several weeks in a screw top bottle, if you keep it in the 'fridge.

Makes 285ml/½ pint (1⅓ cups)
Milk Free

Metric/Imperial		American
2 tbs	plain 85% flour	2 tbs
2 tsp	raw cane sugar	2 tsp
½ tsp	sea salt	½ tsp
2 tsp	dry mustard*	2 tsp
1	free range egg	1
2–3 tbs	lemon juice or white vinegar* (increase if you prefer a stronger taste)	2–3 tbs
140ml/¼ pint	water	⅔ cup
	safflower, sunflower or olive oil (see method)	

1. Sieve the flour, sugar, salt and mustard into a saucepan.
2. Mix to a paste with the egg, then gradually add the water and lemon juice/vinegar. Heat gently, whisking all the time, until the mixture thickens, then cook for a further 4–5 minutes.
3. Allow to cool, then add enough oil to make a thick coating consistency (about 6–7 tablespoons).
4. Put into a screw top bottle or jar and store in the 'fridge.

FRENCH DRESSING

You can vary the amount of oil to lemon juice or vinegar. Use less oil if you like a sharper flavoured dressing. This makes 140ml/¼ pint (⅔ cup). For a gluten-free dressing, omit the mustard.

Milk Free   Egg Free

Metric/Imperial		American
2 tbs	lemon juice	2 tbs
6 tbs	sunflower, safflower or olive oil	6 tbs
	freshly ground sea salt and pepper	
½ level tsp	mustard powder*	½ level tsp
½ level tsp	raw cane sugar	½ level tsp

1. Put the ingredients together in a bowl and whisk. The dressing will separate on standing, so it is a good idea to keep it in a bottle or screw-top jar and shake it well before using.

Note to Cooks

To this you can add fresh herbs*, chives or crushed garlic if wished.

10

Puddings

FRESH FRUIT SALAD

Serves 5–6
Gluten Free   Milk Free   Egg Free

Metric/Imperial		*American*
1	grapefruit, segmented and cut into small pieces	1
2	pears, cored and sliced or ½ small melon, cubed	2
4 slices tinned	pineapple in its own juice	4 slices canned
1 tin	mangoes or 1 fresh mango	1 can
1	pomegranate (optional)	1
1 tbs	raw cane sugar	1 tbs
120ml/4 fl oz	water	½ cup

1. Put the grapefruit into a bowl. Add the pears or melon and mix well to prevent discolouration. Add the other fruit.

2. Dissolve the sugar in the water and pour over.

Note to Cooks

Fresh pineapple is higher in salicylate than tinned.

FIG AND YOGURT DESSERT

Serves 4
Gluten Free   Egg Free

Metric/Imperial		American
115g/4oz	figs (remove strips)	1 cup
2	pears	2
140ml/¼ pint	natural (plain) yogurt	⅔ cup

1. Stew the fruit in a little water and when soft, liquidize together, or mash and purée.
2. Add the yogurt, mix well and serve in individual dishes.

MANGO TOFU SURPRISE

This is simple to make and high in protein.

Serves 3
Gluten Free   Milk Free   Egg Free

Metric/Imperial		*American*
1–2	mangoes or 1 425g/15-oz tin (can)	1–2
1 297g/10½oz pack	silken tofu (soft)	1¼ cups
2 tbs	clear honey* or maple syrup	2 tbs
2 tsp	lemon juice	2 tsp

1. Skin the mangoes, then scrape off the fruit from the stone with a sharp knife. If using tinned (canned) fruit, drain off the syrup.
2. Put the fruit, tofu, honey and lemon juice in a liquidizer and blend together. If you do not have a liquidizer, put the fruit through a sieve then whisk the ingredients together.

INSTANT MANGO DELIGHT

A lovely summer dessert.

Serves 4
Gluten Free   Egg Free

Metric/Imperial		American
1 tin (approx. 430g/15oz)	mangoes	1 can (approx. 2 cups)
2 medium-sized	pears, peeled and cored	2 medium-sized
200g/8oz	fromage frais	8 oz
1 tsp	lime or lemon juice	1 tsp
1 tbs (or to taste)	raw cane sugar	1 tbs (or to taste)

1. Drain the juice from the mangoes, chop the pears and liquidize the fruit until smooth.
2. Mix in the fromage frais, lime juice and sugar. Serve chilled.

INSTANT BANANA WHIP

Serves 4
Gluten Free   Egg Free

Metric/Imperial		American
4	bananas, peeled	4
2 tsp	lemon juice	2 tsp
100g/4oz	quark or fromage frais	4 oz
4 tbs	natural (plain) yogurt	4 tbs
1 tsp	honey* or maple syrup	1 tsp
	chopped nuts to decorate	

1. Chop the bananas and liquidize or mash until smooth. Mix in the lemon juice.
2. If using quark, cream until soft. Beat the yogurt into the quark or fromage frais. Mix well with the bananas and sweeten to taste with the honey or maple syrup.
3. Serve immediately in individual glass dishes. Sprinkle the chopped nuts on top to decorate.

Note to Cooks

This dessert needs to be eaten straight away or the bananas will discolour.

RHUBARB FOOL

Serves 4–5
Gluten Free

Metric/Imperial		American
455g/1lb	rhubarb, chopped	1 pound
	raw cane sugar to taste	
570ml/1 pint	homemade custard sauce (see page 178)	2½ cups
	natural vanilla essence (or use vanilla flavoured sugar)	

1. Cook the rhubarb in a little water for 5–10 minutes until soft, adding sugar to taste. Liquidize the rhubarb when cool and mix with the custard. Chill and serve in individual dishes. Alternatively make it into a rhubarb ice cream, by freezing it for 30 minutes. Then take it out of the freezer and beat well, return it and freeze until set.

INSTANT LEMON PUDDING

Metric/Imperial		American
285ml/½ pint	warm water	1⅓ cups
3 tsp	agar agar	3 tsp
2	free range eggs, lightly boiled	2
2 tbs	raw cane sugar	2 tbs
2 tbs	lemon juice	2 tbs
140ml/¼ pint	safflower or sunflower oil	⅔ cup
	desiccated coconut (optional)	

1. Place the water and agar agar in a liquidizer and blend until agar agar has dissolved and the liquid is foaming.
2. Add the eggs, sugar and lemon juice. Liquidize again.
3. Finally add the oil a little at a time until mixture thickens.
4. Pour into wetted moulds and chill. To serve, garnish with desiccated coconut, or finely chopped nuts.

RHUBARB JELLY

Serves 5–7
Gluten Free   Milk Free   Egg Free

Metric/Imperial		American
455g/1lb	rhubarb	1 pound
425ml/¾ pint	water	2 cups
	raw cane sugar to taste	
1 tsp	ground cinnamon*	1 tsp
	natural red colouring (optional)	
1 tsp	vegetable gelling agent	1 tsp

1. Stew the rhubarb until soft in 285ml/½ pint (1⅛ cups) of water with the sugar, cinnamon and colouring (if used). Allow to cool slightly then liquidize.
2. Mix the gelling agent with 140ml/¼ pint (⅝ cup) of water then add to the puréed rhubarb and liquidize again for a few seconds.
3. Pour into serving dishes and allow to set.
4. Serve with whipped cream or tofu whipped cream.

PINEAPPLE JELLY

Serves 4–6
Gluten Free   Milk Free   Egg Free

Metric/Imperial		American
1 tin (approx. 225g/½ lb)	pineapple pieces in own juice or fresh pineapple	1 can (approx. 1 cup)
1 heaped tsp	vegetable gelling powder	1 heaped tsp
570ml/1 pint	pineapple juice	2½ cups

1. Place the pineapple pieces into a jelly mould or 4–6 individual dishes.
2. Sprinkle the gelling powder onto a little of the cold pineapple juice until completely dissolved.
3. Add to the rest of the juice and heat gently to boiling point for 2 minutes. Pour the hot juice over the fruit and leave to set for 30–60 minutes.
4. Serve with whipped cream, yogurt or tofu whipped cream.

MANGO MERINGUE PUDDING

For a gluten-free recipe, use rice flour instead of wheat flour.

Serves 4–5

Metric/Imperial		*American*
55g/2oz	margarine or unsalted butter	¼ cup
55g/2oz	85% plain flour or rice flour	½ cup
425ml/¾ pint	milk	2 cups
55g/2oz	raw cane sugar	⅓ cup
2	free range eggs, separated	2
1 tin	mangoes, drained	1 can

1. Melt the butter in a pan, stir in the flour, add the milk and whisk until sauce thickens.
2. Take from the heat, and add the sugar, beaten egg yolks and mangoes. Stir quickly.
3. Pour into an oiled pie dish and bake in the oven at 400°F/200°C/gas mark 6 for 20 minutes, or until the pudding is set. Allow to cool.
4. Whisk the egg whites until stiff, adding a little sugar, then spread on top and brown for about 15 minutes in the oven at 300°F/150°C/gas mark 2.

BAKED LEMON PUDDING
(WITH ITS OWN SAUCE)

Serves 3–4

Metric/Imperial		American
55g/2oz	margarine	⅓ cup
85g/3oz	raw cane sugar	½ cup
55g/2oz	85% wheatmeal self-raising flour or rice flour	½ cup
1 large	lemon	1 large
2	free range eggs, separated	2
285ml/½ pint	milk	1⅓ cups

1. Put margarine, sugar, flour, grated lemon rind, and 3 tablespoons of lemon juice in the liquidizer. Add the egg yolks and milk and whisk together.
2. Whisk the egg whites separately until stiff, then fold in to the mixture from the liquidizer.
3. Turn into an oiled 1 litre (2 pint) pie dish. Put pie dish in a larger shallow dish of cold water and bake for 45–60 minutes at 350°F/180°C/gas mark 4 until golden brown and lightly set. A sauce forms below a light sponge. Delicious!

Note to Cooks

If you do not own a liquidizer, cream the margarine with the grated lemon rind. Add the sugar and cream again. Stir in egg yolks, flour and lemon juice, then slowly add the milk like a batter. Continue as described above.

COCONUT SUPREME

For a non-gluten-free recipe, use 55g/2oz (1 cup) of breadcrumbs and 110ml/4 fl oz (⅓ cup) pear juice instead of the millet.

Serves 4
Gluten Free

Metric/Imperial		American
55g/2oz	whole millet	¼ cup
425ml/¾ pint	water	2 cups
2–3 medium to large	pears, cored and thinly sliced	2–3 medium to large
55g/2oz	margarine or butter	¼ cup
55g/2oz	soft raw cane sugar	⅓ cup
2	free range eggs	2
115g/4oz	desiccated coconut	1⅓ cups

1. Cook the millet in water until soft and fluffy. Put into an oiled 570ml/1 pint pie dish. Place the pears on top.
2. Cream the margarine or butter and sugar, whisk in the eggs, and fold in the coconut.
3. Spread on top of the pears.
4. Cook in a slow oven at 300°F/150°C/gas mark 2 for 30–35 minutes until golden brown.

BUTTERSCOTCH BANANAS

Serves 4
Gluten Free   Egg Free

Metric/Imperial		American
6	bananas	6
30g/1oz	butter	2½ tbs
30g/1oz	soft brown muscovado raw cane sugar	2 tbs
1 tsp	grated lemon rind	1 tsp
2 tsp	lemon juice	2 tsp

1. Peel bananas. Cut in half lengthways. Place in oiled ovenproof dish and sprinkle with lemon.
2. Dot with butter and sprinkle with sugar.
3. Cover and bake in the oven at 350°F/180°C/gas mark 4 for 20 minutes.
4. Serve with cream or yogurt, etc.

BANANA SWEET

Gluten Free   Milk Free   Egg Free

Peel one banana per person. Roll in a little melted clear honey* and coat with chopped mixed nuts. Serve as it is or with yogurt, etc.

BAKED MARZIPAN PEARS

Serves 4
Gluten Free   Milk Free

Metric/Imperial		American
115g/4oz	ground hazelnuts	1 cup
4 tsp	lemon juice	4 tsp
2	free range egg yolks	2
4–5 tsp	raw cane sugar	4–5 tsp
4 large	pears (comice are good for this recipe)	4 large
1–2 tbs	raw cane sugar	1–2 tbs

1. Make the marzipan mixture by mixing together the hazelnuts, lemon juice, egg yolk and sugar.
2. Remove the stalks from the pears, then with a teaspoon or apple corer, remove the core from the top, keeping the pears whole.
3. Stuff with the marzipan, and sprinkle with sugar, and bake in a moderate oven at 350°F/180°C/gas mark 4 for 30 minutes. Serve with custard sauce (page 178).

PEAR 'CLAFOUTIS'
(BASED ON A FRENCH RECIPE)

Serves 4
Gluten Free

Metric/Imperial		*American*
455g/1lb	pears, peeled if preferred	1 pound
1 tbs	lemon or grapefruit juice	1 tbs
85–115g/3–4oz	raw cane sugar	½–⅔ cup
2	free range egg yolks	2
1	whole egg	1
115g/4oz	rice flour	¾ cup
115g/4oz	margarine, melted	½ cup
few drops	natural vanilla essence	few drops
200ml/⅓ pint	milk, warmed	¾ cup

1. Preheat the oven to 400°F/200°C/gas mark 6.
2. Slice pears thinly and put into an oiled ovenproof dish. Coat the pears with the juice to stop discolouration.
3. Beat the sugar and egg yolks until mixture becomes white. Add the whole egg and beat again. Add flour and beat in, then the melted margarine, and essence. At the last moment add the warmed milk. Mix well.
4. Pour mixture over the fruit. Cook for 45 minutes until it is set and firm. Eat hot or cold.

CAROB PEAR PUDDING

Serves 4
Milk Free

Metric/Imperial		American
2	free range eggs	2
55g/2oz	muscovado sugar	⅓ cup
55g/2oz	85% self-raising flour	½ cup
30–50g/1–2oz	carob powder	¼–½ cup
3 tbs	water	3 tbs
455g/1lb	dessert pears	1 pound
a few	(English) walnuts or hazelnuts, chopped	a few

1. Whisk together eggs and sugar at maximum speed in electric mixer until double in bulk and light in colour. If you do not have a mixer, separate the eggs and whisk the whites until stiff, then beat in the yolks and sugar.
2. Sift the flour and fold into the egg mixture, including any bran left in the sieve. Add the water to the carob powder, and fold into the sponge mixture.
3. Peel and thinly slice the pears and put into a shallow greased baking dish. Pour sponge mixture on top. Scatter with chopped walnuts (English walnuts) or hazelnuts if liked and bake in the oven at 350°F/180°C/gas mark 4 for 30–40 minutes, until firm to touch. Serve with cream, yogurt, or tofu whipped cream.

DRIED PEARS WITH
GINGERBREAD TOPPING

Serves 4

Metric/Imperial		*American*
225g/½lb	dried pears	1½ cups

Gingerbread:

85g/3oz	black treacle or molasses	3 tbs
55g/2oz	margarine	¼ cup
30g/1oz	raw cane sugar	2½ tbs
115g/4oz	plain 85% flour	1 cup
1 tsp	baking powder	1 tsp
½ tsp	bicarbonate of soda (baking soda)	½ tsp
1 tsp	ground ginger°	1 tsp
1	free range egg	1
5 tbs	milk	5 tbs

1. Rinse the dried pears in boiling water to help wash off the preservative. Leave to soak in fresh water for several hours, then simmer until soft.
2. Warm the treacle, margarine and sugar in a saucepan. Sift the dry ingredients and make a well in the centre. Add the treacle mixture, beaten egg and milk and mix well.
3. Put the pears at the bottom of an ovenproof dish with no liquid. Spread the gingerbread mixture over the top.
4. Bake for 1–1¼ hours at 350°F/180°C/gas mark 4 until it is firm to touch.

5. Serve with custard sauce (see page 178) or yogurt.

Note to Cooks

Replace dried pears with 455–680g/1–1½lb fresh pears, cored and sliced.

PINEAPPLE UPSIDE DOWN CAKE

Serves 4–6

Metric/Imperial		American
2 tbs	clear honey*	2 tbs
4–6 slices	pineapple, canned in own juice (keep juice)	4–6 slices
1 tbs	muscovado sugar	1 tbs
170g/6oz	margarine	⅔ cup
85g/3oz	muscovado sugar	½ cup
3	free range eggs, beaten	3
170g/6oz	wholemeal or 85% self-raising flour	1½ cups
55g/2oz	carob powder (optional)	½ cup
	milk, yogurt or pineapple juice	

1. Well oil a 20cm (8-inch) round cake tin. Spread honey over base and arrange pineapple rings on top. Sprinkle 1 tablespoon of sugar over pineapple.
2. Cream margarine and sugar until light and fluffy. Gradually add beaten eggs and fold in sifted flour and carob powder, if used, mixed together.
3. Add enough liquid to give dropping consistency. Spread over pineapple. Bake at 350°F/180°C/gas mark 4 for 50 minutes to 1 hour until firm to the touch.
4. Carefully turn out on to a plate and serve hot with custard sauce etc. (see page 178), or eat cold with yogurt or cream, etc.

Note to Cooks

Replace pineapple with 2 to 3 pears, halved. Fill the core hole with chopped figs.

UNCOOKED LEMON CHEESECAKE

Serves 4–6

Metric/Imperial		American
170g/6oz	digestive biscuits (Graham crackers) or semi-sweet or ryvita biscuits	1¾ cups
85g/3oz	unsalted butter	⅓ cup
225g/½ lb	quark	1 cup
4 tbs	homemade lemon curd	4 tbs
140ml/¼ pint	double (heavy) cream, whipped	⅔ cup

1. Crush digestive biscuits (Graham crackers) between two pieces of greaseproof (parchment) paper with a rolling pin. Melt butter and mix with biscuit crumbs. Press into a fluted flan tin, or flat ring on a flat dish. Leave to cool until firm.
2. Meanwhile, beat in the 4 tablespoons of lemon curd with the quark, and fold in the cream.
3. Smooth on to prepared flan, and leave to set.

PINEAPPLE CHEESE TART

Serves 4–6

Metric/Imperial		*American*
340g/12oz	fromage frais	12oz
2 tbs	raw cane sugar	2 tbs
2	free range eggs, beaten	2
4 slices	pineapple, fresh or tinned (canned)	4 slices
1 20cm (8-in)	flan case (see page 192)	1 8-in

1. Mix together the fromage frais, raw cane sugar and eggs and beat until smooth.
2. Cut three of the pineapple slices into small pieces and stir carefully into the cheese mixture.
3. Put into the flan case and bake at 350°F/180°C/gas mark 4 for 35–40 minutes or until firm to the touch.
4. Cut the fourth slice of pineapple into sections and decorate the top of the tart.

Note to Cooks

This recipe is also tasty if you use 175g/6oz fromage frais and 140ml/5oz yogurt.

PEAR AND MANGO CRUMBLE

Serves 4–5
Egg Free

Metric/Imperial		American
1–2	pears, peeled and sliced	1–2
1 tin	mangoes, drained	1 can
(approx.		(approx.
425g/15oz)		2 cups)

For the crumble:

115g/4oz	85% flour	1 cup
55g/2oz	rolled oats	2oz
55g/2oz	soft brown sugar	⅓ cup
85g/3oz	margarine or butter	⅓ cup
30g/1oz	hazelnuts, chopped	¼ cup
	and roasted (optional)	

1. Put the sliced pears and mangoes into a pie dish.
2. To make the crumble, combine the flour, oats, sugar and margarine or butter in a bowl. Rub in the fat then fork in the hazelnuts.
3. Sprinkle the mixture over the fruit and press down. Bake at 350°F/180°C/gas mark 4 for 40 minutes or until the crumble has browned. Serve with custard, yogurt or ice cream.

Notes to Cooks

For a variation, substitute 455g/1lb (1 pound) of cooked rhubarb with two bananas (chopped) instead of the pear and mango.

For a gluten-free topping, see Soya Crumble (page 187).

FIG AND NUT SLICE

Makes 6–9 slices
Egg Free

Metric/Imperial		*American*
170g/6oz	margarine	⅔ cup
340g/¾lb	85% self-raising wheatmeal flour	3 cups
3 tbs	cold water	3 tbs

For the filling:

340g/¾lb	figs, strigged	2½ cups
140ml/¼ pint	water	⅔ cup
115g/4oz	chopped (English) walnuts or hazelnuts	¾ cup

1. Grease an 18cm/7-in square baking tin. Preheat the oven to 350°F/180°C/gas mark 4.
2. Make the pastry by rubbing the fat into the flour and adding the water to make a dough. Chill in the 'fridge while making the filling.
3. Cut the figs into small pieces and simmer gently in the water for 10–15 minutes until soft. Mash into a purée.
4. Roll out half the dough on a floured board and line the tin. Add chopped nuts to the fig mixture and spread on top of pastry. Roll out the remaining dough and place on top. Trim and press down firmly, then prick with a fork.
5. Bake for 30 minutes in the preheated oven.
6. Cool in the tin and cut into slices. Eat for tea, or serve hot with custard or yogurt.

Hyperactive Child

Note to Cooks

Rinse dried fruit well in boiling water, especially if sulphur dioxide or mineral oil has been used.

MILLET MILK PUDDING

Serves 4
Gluten Free   Egg Free

Metric/Imperial		*American*
85–115g/3–4oz	dried pears	½–¾ cup
55g/2oz	millet, whole or (1 scant cup) flaked	¼ cup
570ml/1 pint	milk	2½ cups
1	bay leaf (optional)*	1

1. Cut the pears into small pieces with scissors. Do not use the core unless soft. Wash the millet (whole only). Wash the pears through a sieve with hot water to help remove preservative.
2. Heat the milk. Add the millet and pears to the hot milk. Bring to the boil, simmer until soft and fluffy and the milk has absorbed, about 25–30 minutes.
3. Transfer to an oiled ovenproof dish. Lay the bay leaf on the top if used and cook at 350°F/180°C/gas mark 4 for 30–40 minutes until set and well browned.

Notes to Cooks

1. Use chopped dates* or figs instead of dried pears, but do not cook these in the milk first. Arrange the figs and dates* in the oiled ovenproof dish and pour the hot milk and softened millet on top.
2. Added sugar should not be necessary but may be added if desired.
3. Whole brown rice may be used instead of millet.

Hyperactive Child

4. For extra nourishment, one or two eggs may be added
   before putting the pudding in the oven, either with or
   without fruit. Eat hot or cold. (Now not egg free.)

BAKED CUSTARD

Serves 4
Grain Free   Gluten Free

Metric/Imperial		American
3	free range eggs	3
2 tsp	raw cane sugar	2 tsp
425ml/¾ pint	milk	2 cups
1	bay leaf* or grated nutmeg* (optional)	1

1. Beat eggs and raw cane sugar very well in an oven-proof dish. Gradually add milk, beating all the time. Place bay leaf on the top or sprinkle a little grated nutmeg over.
2. Stand dish in a larger dish (eg. roasting pan) of cold water as custard must not boil.
3. Cook in warm oven at 325°F/170°C/gas mark 3 for 45–60 minutes until set. Serve hot or cold, on its own or with fruit.

CARAMEL CUSTARD

Serves 4
Gluten Free

Use the same quantities of ingredients as for Baked Custard but with only 1 tsp of sugar. Mix in a basin as described above.

1. Heat the oven. Put an ovenproof dish (such as a soufflé dish) in to warm.
2. Warm the milk before adding to the egg mixture.

For the caramel:

1. Slowly heat 2 tbs of raw cane sugar with 1 tbs of water in a saucepan until it melts and changes colour. Quickly coat the sides of the warmed dish with caramel and add the well-beaten mixture. Cook using the same method as above.
2. Cook and chill. About 1 hour before serving, remove from the refrigerator and free edges with a knife. Carefully turn out onto a serving plate.

CUSTARD SAUCE

Serves 4
Gluten Free

Metric/Imperial		American
30g/1oz	rice (or maize*) flour	1oz
30g/1oz	raw cane sugar	1oz
570ml/1 pint	milk	2½ cups
2	free range egg yolks	2
a few drops	vanilla essence	a few drops
	(or a vanilla pod or a few strips of lemon rind to flavour)	

1. Whisk the flour and sugar into the milk and heat until it thickens, stirring all the time. As it starts to boil, continue to cook for 3 minutes.
2. Quickly whisk in the egg yolks and simmer for a further minute to ensure that the eggs are cooked. Add vanilla essence if not using the other flavouring methods.

Note to Cooks

Use the egg whites to make Macaroons (see page 201) or Coconut Pyramids (see page 200).

TOFU WHIPPED CREAM

Tofu, or soybean curd, is high in protein, low in fats, yet rich in polyunsaturates. You can buy it in most health shops. This makes a delicious cream.

Serves 4–6
Gluten Free   Milk Free   Egg Free

Metric/Imperial		American
1 297g/10½oz pack	silken tofu, soft	1¼ cups
4 tbs	sunflower oil	4 tbs
1 tbs	honey* or ground raw cane sugar	1 tbs
½ tsp	lemon juice	½ tsp
1 tsp	natural vanilla essence	1 tsp

1. Whisk or liquidize the ingredients together to make a thick cream.
2. Add puréed fruit of choice to this to make a delicious sweet.

NUT CREAM

Gluten Free   Milk Free   Egg Free

Put nuts of your choice in a liquidizer and add water to make a spreading consistency. Add more water to make a thinner cream for topping fruit etc.

See also 'Drinks', pages 264–74.

YOGURT ICE CREAM

Gluten Free   Egg Free

Metric/Imperial		American
140ml/¼ pint	double (heavy) cream	⅔ cup
285ml/½ pint	homemade yogurt	1⅓ cups
	raw cane sugar to taste	
225g/½lb	puréed allowed fruit such as: pears, rhubarb, figs, guavas, pineapple (chopped small), mangoes or passion fruit or chopped (English) walnuts or hazelnuts	2 cups

1. Whip the cream until stiff, and then add to the yogurt.
2. Stir in raw cane sugar to taste.
3. Mix all ingredients well, then freeze. Remove after 1 hour and remix with a fork. Replace for a final freeze.

CAROB ICE CREAM

Makes a soft ice cream.

Gluten Free   Egg Free

Metric/Imperial		American
1 large (411g/ 14.5oz) tin	evaporated milk, chilled	1 large can
1 rounded tbs	carob powder, sieved	1 rounded tbs
4 tbs	raw cane sugar	4 tbs
4 tbs	water	4 tbs

1. Chill evaporated milk for 2 hours in a 'fridge or ½ hour in a freezer.
2. Mix carob powder, raw cane sugar and water.
3. Place evaporated milk in a fairly large bowl and beat until thick and nearly treble the quantity.
4. Fold in the carob mixture until well mixed.
5. Place in two plastic ice cream containers and freeze.
6. Remove from freezer about 10 minutes before serving.

Note to Cooks

Replace the carob powder with 115g/4oz ground hazelnuts.

11

Breads and Cakes

IF YOU have been using refined flours, some children may find the transition to wholemeal flours rather drastic. You could try organic white and 85% flours instead. Note that organic flour does not contain pesticide residues which may be present in ordinary wholemeal flours.

When sieving these flours the bran will be left behind. You can either add this to the sieved flour or sprinkle it over the bottom of the baking tin.

Few people realize that one third of the grain is removed in the milling of white flour, and that this is the part which contains vitamin E, the B vitamins, and essential minerals such as calcium, zinc, magnesium, manganese, copper and iron. The manufacturers are required by law to put back only four – vitamin B_1 (thiamine), vitamin B_3 (niacin), calcium in the form of chalk, and iron. The other important B vitamins (including vitamin B_6 (pyridoxine) and folic acid) vitamin E, the other minerals and fibre are excluded.

HOMEMADE WHOLEMEAL (WHOLEWHEAT) BREAD

Milk Free   Egg Free

Metric/Imperial		American
680g/1½lb	100% wholemeal (wholewheat) flour	1½ pounds
2 tsp	sea salt	2 tsp
30g/1oz	fresh yeast or 15g/½oz (1 heaped tbs) dried yeast	2½ tbs
2 tsp	raw cane sugar	2 tsp
2 tbs	oil	2 tbs
425ml/¾ pint	warm water	2 cups

1. Put the flour and salt into a warmed bowl.
2. Put the warm water into another bowl, blend in the yeast and sugar and leave until frothy.
3. Add this to the flour mixture, then mix in the oil. Mix well together, then tip on to a floured board, and knead for 2–3 minutes until it feels firm and elastic and no longer sticky.
4. Cover, and leave for half an hour in a warm place before dividing.
5. Divide into 2 or 3 pieces and put into oiled tins – more fun if the tins are all different, for instance you can buy animal shapes.
6. Cover with a clean tea towel, or greased polythene bag, and leave in a warm place until the dough has doubled in size.

7. Bake at 400°F/200°C/gas mark 6 for 10 minutes, then reduce the heat to 350°F/180°C/gas mark 4 for a further 25–35 minutes. If the bread is cooked it should sound hollow when tapped on the base with the knuckles.
8. When cooked, turn out onto a wire rack to cool.

Note to Cooks

For a lighter loaf use 340g/¾lb (¾ pound) unbleached white and the same amount again of 100% wholemeal (wholewheat) flour.

Breads and Cakes

YEAST FREE POTATO BREAD

Gluten Free   Milk Free

Metric/Imperial		American
115g/4oz	potato farina (flour)	¾ cup
2 heaped tbs	soya (soy) flour	2 heaped tbs
2 level tsp	grain-free baking powder	2 level tsp
pinch	sea salt	pinch
30g/1oz	milk-free margarine or 1 tbs oil	2½ tbs
1 tsp	raw cane sugar	1 tsp
1	free range egg, beaten	1
120ml/4 fl oz	water	½ cup

1. Sieve together potato farina, soya (soy) flour, baking powder and salt. Rub in margarine or oil and then add sugar and stir.
2. Add beaten egg and water and whisk or beat to a smooth batter.
3. Put into a greased or oiled 455g/1lb lined loaf tin and bake at 400°F/200°C/gas mark 6 for about 35 minutes.
4. Turn out on to a wire rack to cool.

Note to Cooks

A little soya (soy) bran could be added to this recipe to give dietary fibre.

Reproduced by kind permission of Foodwatch.

SOYA CRUMBLE

Gluten Free   Milk Free   Egg Free

Metric/Imperial		American
225g/½lb	soya (soy) flour	2 cups
4 tbs	oil	4 tbs
	grated rind of ½ lemon	
pinch	sea salt	pinch
	cold water as required	

1. Mix flour with oil, lemon rind and salt. Mix well with a fork. Add just enough cold water to hold dough together but let it stay crumbly.
2. Press into a 23cm (9-inch) flan dish and bake at 350°F/ 180°C/gas mark 4 for 15 minutes.
3. When cold, crumble over any stewed or fresh 'safe' fruit.

Note to Cooks

For a sweet crumble add 55g/2oz (⅓ cup) of raw cane sugar.

GLUTEN-FREE PASTRY

Gluten Free

Metric/Imperial		*American*
225g/½lb	rice flour	1½ cups
30g/1oz	soya (soy) flour	¼ cup
55g/2oz	margarine	¼ cup
55g/2oz	vegetable fat	¼ cup
½ tsp	gluten-free baking powder (optional)	½ tsp
1	free range egg (approximately 40g)	1
1 little	milk	a little

1. Place rice flour, soya (soy) flour, margarine, fat and baking powder into a bowl. Rub all together until mixture resembles breadcrumbs.
2. Add beaten egg and enough milk to form a soft dough. Roll out and bake at 435°F/225°C/gas mark 7 for 10–12 minutes (tarts) or 35–40 minutes (pies).

Note to Cooks

Pastry can be pressed in dish in place of rolling, or used as a crumble.

GLUTEN-FREE BAKING POWDER

Metric/Imperial		American
100g/4oz	rice flour	4oz
50g/2oz	bicarbonate of soda	2oz
50g/2oz	tartaric acid	2oz

1. Mix ingredients together. Sieve several times then store in a screw-top jar.

GLUTEN-FREE BISCUITS

Makes 14–16
Gluten Free

Metric/Imperial		American
85g/3oz	margarine or butter	⅓ cup
200g/7oz	rice flour	1½ cups less 1½ tbs
30g/1oz	soya (soy) flour	¼ cup
pinch	sea salt	pinch
1	free range egg	1
60g/2½oz	raw cane sugar	⅓ cup + 1 tbs

1. Either rub margarine or butter into all dry ingredients together and bind with beaten egg, or cream fat and sugar together, add beaten egg and all other ingredients. Make into a ball and add a little milk if too dry.
2. Shape into approximately teaspoon-sized balls with your hands and flatten onto an oiled baking sheet to make about 16 rounds.
3. Bake at 350°F/180°C/gas mark 4 for 15–20 minutes until golden brown. Two biscuits can be sandwiched together to make cream biscuits using nut cream (see page 180).

Note to Cooks

Any of the following may be added to the above ingredients:

1. 30g/1oz (⅓ cup) coconut.
2. 1 tsp ginger*.
3. 1 tbs carob powder, sifted.
4. 55g/2oz (⅓ cup) dates* or figs, finely chopped.

SHORTCRUST PASTRY

This recipe makes enough pastry for a 23–25cm (9–10-in) flan case. For a 20cm (8-in) flan case use 170g/6oz (1 cup) flour and 85g/3oz (⅓ cup) margarine.

Egg Free

Metric/Imperial		American
225g/½lb	plain 100% wholemeal or 85% wheatmeal flour	2 cups
pinch	sea salt	pinch
2 level tsp	baking powder	2 level tsp
115g/4oz	margarine or 55g/2oz (¼ cup) margarine and 55g/2oz (¼ cup) vegetable fat	½ cup
	cold water to mix, about 2 tbs	

1. Sift together flour, salt and baking powder.
2. Rub in fat until mixture resembles fine breadcrumbs. Add water slowly and mix carefully to make a ball of dough.
3. Rest the pastry in the refrigerator for 20–30 minutes. Wrap carefully in a polythene bag or clingfilm.
4. Roll out on floured board, taking care as wholemeal pastry is more crumbly than white flour pastry.

OATCAKES

Makes 12 large, 20 small
Egg Free

Metric/Imperial		American
170g/6oz	medium oatmeal	1½ cups
55g/2oz	wholemeal or 85% flour	½ cup
1 tsp	baking powder	1 tsp
½ tsp	sea salt	½ tsp
85g/3oz	vegetable margarine	⅓ cup
3 tbs	water	3 tbs
	sunflower or sesame seeds	

1. Combine the oatmeal, wholemeal (wholewheat) flour, baking powder and salt.
2. Put the margarine and water in a saucepan and bring to the boil.
3. Pour on to the dry ingredients and mix to a soft dough, adding more boiling water if necessary.
4. Roll out thinly on a board dusted with oatmeal. Sprinkle with sesame or sunflower seeds and press well down on to the dough with the rolling pin.
5. Cut into triangles and bake for 20 minutes at 350°F/180°C/gas mark 4, or cook on a moderately hot griddle (skillet), until oatcakes start to curl at the edges.

YOGURT SCONES

Makes 12
Egg Free

Metric/Imperial		American
225g/½lb	wholemeal (wholewheat) or 85% flour	2 cups
1 level tsp	bicarbonate of soda (baking soda) and 1 level tsp cream of tartar (or 2–3 tsp baking powder)	1 level tsp
½ tsp	sea salt	½ tsp
55g/2oz	margarine	¼ cup
140ml/¼ pint	natural (plain) cow's or goat's yogurt	⅔ cup

1. Sift together the dry ingredients.
2. Rub in the margarine, then add the yogurt quickly, mixing with a knife to make a soft dough.
3. Roll out to about 1cm (½ inch) thickness. Cut with 6cm (2½ inch) diameter cutter.
4. Bake in a hot oven at 425°F/220°C/gas mark 7 for 10–12 minutes. Makes 12 scones. Best eaten fresh, but can be frozen.

SESAME THINS

These are lovely served with soup or cheese, and you can vary the topping by using poppy or celery seeds.

Makes 40–45
Egg Free

Metric/Imperial		American
225g/½lb	plain wholemeal or 85% flour	2 cups
55g/2oz	rice flour	3 tbs
2 level tsp	raw cane sugar	2 level tsp
½ level tsp	bicarbonate of soda (baking soda)	½ level tsp
½ level tsp	sea salt	½ level tsp
85g/3oz	margarine or butter	⅓ cup
3–4 tbs	water	3–4 tbs
1 tbs	lemon or lime juice	1 tbs

Topping:

4 tbs	sesame or sunflower seeds oil for coating	4 tbs

1. Put the flours, sugar, bicarbonate of soda (baking soda) and salt into a basin.
2. Rub in the margarine until it resembles fine breadcrumbs.
3. Add the water and lemon juice, mix to a sconelike dough, then roll out until it is very thin.

Breads and Cakes

4. Brush the dough with oil. Sprinkle with sesame seeds, and press them onto the dough with the rolling pin. Cut out with a circular biscuit cutter 5cm (2 in) in diameter. Put biscuits onto a greased tray.

5. Bake in a moderate oven at 375°F/190°C/gas mark 5 for about 15–20 minutes or until crisp and lightly brown. Cool on a rack and store in an airtight tin.

OAT CRUNCHIES

Makes 24–26
Egg Free

Metric/Imperial		American
115g/4oz	margarine	½ cup
85g/3oz	raw cane sugar	½ cup
1 tsp	honey* or treacle	1 tsp
1 tsp	bicarbonate of soda (baking soda) stirred into a tsp boiling water	1 tsp
115g/4oz	oats	1 cup
115g/4oz	85% self-raising flour	1 cup

1. Melt the margarine, sugar, honey and bicarbonate of soda (baking soda) in a pan. Stir in the oats and flour and mix well.
2. Place teaspoons of the mixture on to a greased baking sheet and flatten into rounds.
3. Bake at 350°F/180°C/gas mark 4 for 20 minutes. These are quick and easy to make and are delicious.

QUICK LEMON BUNS

Makes 12–14

Metric/Imperial		*American*
170g/6oz	85% self-raising flour	1½ cups
115g/4oz	margarine, softened	½ cup
85g/3oz	raw cane sugar	½ cup
2	free range eggs	2
	grated rind of 1 lemon	
1 tsp	baking powder	1 tsp
4 tbs	milk	4 tbs

Topping:

1 tsp	honey*	1 tsp
a little	lemon juice	a little
	desiccated coconut	

1. Sift flours and baking powder, put all cake ingredients into a bowl and mix well.
2. Have bun tins ready with the baking cases standing inside them, and spoon mixture equally into them.
3. Bake in a preheated oven at 375°F/190°C/gas mark 5 for approximately 20 minutes.
4. To make the topping, mix the honey with a little lemon juice to make a thin liquid. Spread over cooled buns to give glaze effect, and sprinkle with desiccated coconut.

Note to Cooks

Substitute the topping with No-Sugar Icing (page 220).

QUICK CAROB BUNS

Makes 8

Metric/Imperial		American
115g/4oz	margarine or butter	½ cup
225g/½lb	85% wheatmeal self-raising flour or plain wholemeal flour with ½ tsp baking powder	2 cups
85g/3oz	raw cane sugar	½ cup
30–55g/1–2oz	carob powder	¼–½ cup
1	free range egg	1
	allowed jam or marmalade	
a little	milk for glaze	a little

1. Rub the margarine or butter into the flour. Add the sugar and carob. Beat the egg and add to the mixture to make a stiff paste.
2. Put the mixture into bun tins, make a hole in the middle of each bun, and put in about ½ tsp of allowed marmalade or jam. Draw mixture over the top of jam or marmalade and seal.
3. Brush with milk and bake for 15 minutes at 375°F/190°C/gas mark 5.

Note to Cooks

You can replace the carob powder with 55g/2oz (⅓ cup) chopped dates* or figs, or 55g/2oz (⅔ cup) coconut.

COCONUT PYRAMIDS

Makes 6
Gluten Free   Milk Free

Metric/Imperial		American
115g/4oz	desiccated coconut	1⅓ cups
2 tbs	ground demerara sugar	2 tbs
2	free range egg whites	2

1. Combine the above ingredients. The mixture should be stiff enough to make into pyramid shapes. Add a little more coconut if needed.
2. Use 1 tablespoon of mixture to make each shape.
3. Put shapes into oiled bun cases or on to rice paper, and bake in a slow oven at 300°F/150°C/gas mark 2 for approximately 20 minutes.

HAZELNUT MACAROONS

Makes 6
Gluten Free   Milk Free

Metric/Imperial		American
115g/4oz	ground hazelnuts	¾ cup
85g/3oz	ground raw cane sugar	½ cup
2 small	free range egg whites	2 small
	whole hazelnuts to decorate	

1. Mix the above ingredients except the whole nuts. If you like a crispy top, save some egg white to brush the tops.
2. Oil and flour a baking tray, shaking off excess flour, or line with rice paper.
3. Put teaspoons of mixture on to the tray, and place a whole hazelnut in the middle of each.
4. Bake in a moderate oven at 350°F/180°C/gas mark 4 for 15–20 minutes.

Note to Cooks

You can vary the mixture by using 85g/3oz (⅔ cup) hazelnuts, and 30g/1oz (3 tbs) brazil or walnuts.

FLAPJACKS

Makes 9–10
Egg Free

Metric/Imperial		American
140g/5oz	margarine	½ cup + 2½ tbs
55–85g/2–3oz	raw cane sugar	⅓–½ cup
1 tbs	black treacle (or molasses*)	1 tbs
225g/½lb	rolled oats	2 cups

1. Melt margarine, sugar and molasses slowly in a large saucepan and add oats.
2. Spread into an oiled shallow 18cm/7-in square baking tin and bake at 375°F/190°C/gas mark 5 for approximately 20–25 minutes.
3. Mark into squares while still hot, and remove from tin when cold. For special occasions put into cake cases.

COCONUT BARS

Makes 9–12 bars

Metric/Imperial		*American*
Pastry:		
170g/6oz	85% plain flour	1½ cups
85g/3oz	margarine or unsalted butter	⅓ cup
55g/2oz	raw cane sugar	⅓ cup

1. Put the flour, margarine, and sugar into a bowl and mix into a dough.
2. Press mixture into an oiled 18cm/7-in square tin and bake in the oven at 350°F/180°C/gas mark 4 for approximately 20 minutes.

Topping:		
2	free range egg whites	2
55g/2oz	raw cane sugar	⅓ cup
115g/4oz	desiccated coconut allowed jam	1⅓ cups

1. Whisk egg whites until stiff, and add remaining ingredients. Spread a little 'safe' jam if desired evenly on top of pastry mixture, then cover with the coconut topping.

2. Return to the oven for a further 25–30 minutes, or until top is golden brown. Cool in the tin and cut into slices when cold.

Note to Cooks

Replace the coconut with chopped walnuts or hazelnuts.

SUNFLOWER/SESAME BARS

For a milk free recipe use soya (soy) milk powder.

Makes 12
Gluten Free   Egg Free

Metric/Imperial		*American*
55g/2oz	sunflower seeds	½ cup
55g/2oz	sesame seeds	½ cup
55g/2oz	desiccated coconut	⅔ cup
1 tbs	dried milk powder (soya if necessary)	1 tbs
2 tbs	clear honey*	2 tbs

1. Mix all ingredients together thoroughly with a fork and put into an oiled ovenproof dish 18cm (7 inches) square.
2. Bake in the oven at 350°F/180°C/gas mark 4 for 20 minutes. While still warm score into 12 pieces.

Note to Cooks

Use any safe nuts or seeds as desired.

GINGERBREAD MEN

Makes 6
Egg Free

Metric/Imperial		American
115g/4oz	margarine	½ cup
225g/½lb	85% flour	2 cups
85g/3oz	demerara or muscovado sugar	½ cup
2 tbs	black treacle (or molasses*)	2 tbs
1 tsp	ginger*	1 tsp
2 tsp	lemon juice	2 tsp
pieces of	date or nuts for decoration	pieces of

1. Rub the margarine into the flour. Add the sugar, treacle or molasses, ginger and juice to make a firm dough. Put the dough in the refrigerator for 30 minutes to make it easier to roll out.

2. Roll out on a floured board and cut into shapes. If you do not have a gingerbread man shape, cut out a greaseproof paper shape first, place it on the dough and cut around it. Use an egg slice to put the men on a floured baking sheet, and add pieces of date for eyes, nose, mouth and buttons.

3. Bake at 350°F/180°C/gas mark 4 for about 10–15 minutes. Allow to cool but remove from the tin while still warm.

Note to Cooks

You can also use this recipe to make 28 ginger biscuits.

Hyperactive Child

HOT CROSS BUNS

Makes 12–14

Metric/Imperial		American
30g/1oz	fresh yeast or 1 level tbs dried yeast plus 1 tsp demerara sugar	2½ tbs
285ml/½ pint	warm milk and water mixed	1⅓ cups
455g/1lb	85% or organic white flour	4 cups
½ level tsp	sea salt	½ level tsp
½ level tsp	ground cinnamon*	½ level tsp
¼ level tsp	ground nutmeg*	¼ level tsp
55g/2oz	demerara sugar	⅓ cup
1	free range egg	1
55g/2oz	margarine or butter, melted	¼ cup
115g/4oz	chopped dried pears or figs or both	⅔ cup
55g/2oz	chopped crystallized lemon peel	⅓ cup

Glaze:

1 tbs	water	1 tbs
1 tbs	demerara sugar, boiled together until the sugar is dissolved	1 tbs

1. Stir fresh yeast into warmed milk and water. For dried yeast stir sugar into milk mixture and sprinkle on dried yeast, leaving for 10 minutes until frothy.

2. Mix flour, salt, spices and sugar in a warmed mixing bowl. When the yeast is frothy add this to the flour with the egg, melted butter, fruit and peel. Mix well, then leave covered with a cloth in a warm place until doubled in size.

3. When risen turn on to a floured board and divide into 12–14 equal portions.

4. Put on to greased baking tins and leave in a warm place until risen.

5. Make rice paper or pastry crosses and put on the buns.

6. Bake in the centre of a hot oven at 425°F/220°C/gas mark 7 for 15–20 minutes.

7. Brush the glaze over the buns while they are hot.

Note to Cooks

Crystallized lemon peel is obtainable from health food stores or make your own (see page 205).

HERBED CHEESE BREAD

Metric/Imperial		American
225g/½lb	self-raising 85% flour	2 cups
	freshly ground pepper	
	and sea salt	
1 level tsp	mustard powder*	1 level tsp
1 level tbs	chopped fresh chives	1 level tbs
1 level tbs	chopped fresh parsley	1 level tbs
	or 1 tsp dried	
115g/4oz	cheddar cheese, grated	1 cup
30g/1oz	unsalted butter or	2½ tbs
	margarine	
1	free range egg, beaten	1
140ml/¼ pint	water	⅔ cup

1. Grease a 455g/1lb loaf tin. Sift the flour.
2. Mix the flour, salt, pepper, mustard, herbs and cheese together in a bowl.
3. Melt the butter and add to the flour with the egg and water. Mix well to form a soft dropping consistency, adding more water if necessary.
4. Spoon into prepared tin and bake in the oven at 375°F/190°C/gas mark 5 for 45 minutes or until golden brown. Leave to cool on a wire rack. Serve sliced and buttered.

PEAR, DATE AND WALNUT LOAF

Metric/Imperial		American
1	pear, peeled	1
85g/3oz	dates	½ cup
85g/3oz	(English) walnuts	⅔ cup
1½ tsp	baking powder	1½ tsp
225g/8oz	organic white or 85% flour	2 cups
115g/4oz	margarine or butter	½ cup
115g/4oz	soft brown sugar	⅔ cup
2	free range eggs, beaten	2
1 tbs	milk	1 tbs

1. Heat the oven to 350°F/180°C/gas mark 4 and prepare a 900g/2-lb (2-pound) loaf tin by lining with oiled, greaseproof paper.
2. Chop the pear, dates and walnuts fairly finely.
3. In a separate bowl, sift the baking powder into the flour, then rub in the fat until the mixture resembles fine breadcrumbs. Add the sugar, eggs and milk, mixing well. Tip in the prepared fruit and mix again.
4. Put the mixture into the loaf tin and bake for 1 hour until the loaf is springy to the touch.

Note to Cooks

For a variation, substitute a mashed banana for the pear.

CARROT CAKE

Metric/Imperial		American
85g/3oz	margarine or butter	½ cup
85g/3oz	soft brown sugar	1 cup
2	free range eggs	2
225g/8oz	85% self-raising flour	1½ cups
1 tsp	baking powder	1 tsp
1 tsp	ground cinnamon*	1 tsp
pinch	nutmeg*	pinch
115g/4oz	grated carrots	⅔ cup
2	ripe bananas, mashed	2

1. Cream the fat with the sugar until fluffy. Gradually beat in the eggs, adding a little flour if the mixture seems likely to curdle.
2. Sieve together the flour, baking powder, cinnamon and nutmeg, and fold gently into the creamed mixture.
3. Fold in the grated carrot and mashed banana, and mix carefully.
4. Put the mixture into an oiled 18cm/7-in cake tin and bake at 350°F/180°C/gas mark 4 for 1 hour.

Note to Cooks

Fudge Icing makes a delicious topping (see page 221).

STICKY LIME CAKE

This is a delicious, moist cake.

Serves 6

Metric/Imperial		*American*
115g/4oz	butter or margarine	½ cup
115g/4oz	soft brown demerara sugar	⅔ cup
2	free range eggs	2
170g/6oz	85% self-raising flour	1½ cups
1–2 tbs	milk (to mix)	1–2 tbs

For the lime syrup:

juice of 1	lime (about 2 tbs), strained	juice of 1
55g/2oz	raw cane sugar	¼ cup

1. Heat the oven to 350°F/180°C/gas mark 4.
2. Cream together the fat and sugar until light and fluffy.
3. Whisk the eggs and gradually stir into the creamed mix, a little at a time, adding small amounts of flour with the last of the egg.
4. Fold in the remaining flour, using a metal spoon, adding the milk to make a soft dropping consistency.
5. Spoon the mixture into an oiled 17.5cm/7-in shallow cake tin. Cook in the centre of the oven for 30–35 minutes until risen and lightly browned. Leave in the tin.
6. Meanwhile heat gently the strained lime juice and sugar in a saucepan until the sugar has dissolved. Prick the hot cake all over with a fork or cocktail stick, and spoon over the hot syrup. Leave the cake in the tin to cool and remove carefully when cold.

Hyperactive Child

YOGURT CAKE

Metric/Imperial		American
115g/4oz	yogurt	4oz
115g/4oz	raw cane sugar	½ cup
55ml/2 fl oz	oil	¼ cup
3	free range eggs, beaten	3
170g/6oz	85% self-raising flour, sifted	1 cup

1. Oil an 18cm/7-in cake tin and preheat the oven to 350°F/180°C/gas mark 4.
2. Put the yogurt, raw cane sugar, oil and eggs into a basin and mix well together. Fold in the sifted flour.
3. Bake for approximately 40 minutes until golden brown.
4. Leave to cool, then slice the cake horizontally and spread with Creamy Filling (see page 222).

Note to Cooks

Once the cake has been filled, keep in a cool place and eat the same day.

BASIC SPONGE/PUDDING RECIPE

Makes 1 20cm (8-in) cake or 32 small cakes
Gluten Free   Milk Free

Metric/Imperial		American
170g/6oz	milk-free margarine	⅔ cup
115g/4oz	raw cane sugar, vanilla flavoured	⅔ cup
3	free range eggs	3
85g/3oz	potato flour	¾ cup less 1½ tbs
85g/3oz	rice flour	¾ cup less 1½ tbs
30g/1oz	soya (soy) flour	¼ cup
3 heaped tsp	wheat-free baking powder	3 heaped tsp
a little	water	a little

1. Oil two 20cm/8-inch round cake tins.
2. Cream margarine and sugar until light and fluffy. Add beaten eggs, slowly, one at a time. Stir sifted flours and baking powder together and fold into mixture. Add water if necessary to make a dropping consistency.
3. Bake at 350°F/180°C/gas mark 4 for approximately 20 minutes. Will also make 32 small cakes.

Note to Cooks

Variations:

1. Add 55g/2oz (½ cup) carob powder, sieved.
2. Add 55–85g/2–3oz (¼–⅔ cup) chopped nuts or peel.
3. Filling: Use marzipan paste recipe on page 219.
4. Makes a delicious, good size sponge pudding. Use a 1 litre/2 pint basin.
5. Cream cakes: Make 32 small cakes with basic mixture, and bake for 10–15 minutes. Cool, cut off the tops and fill with any 'safe' filling of choice.

CELEBRATION CAKE

Metric/Imperial		American
225g/½lb	margarine or butter	1 cup
225g/½lb	muscovado sugar	1⅛ cups
4 large	free range eggs	4 large
340g/¾lb	plain 85% wheatmeal flour	3 cups
pinch	sea salt	pinch
1 level tsp	baking powder	1 level tsp
170g/6oz	crystallized pineapple, chopped	1 cup
115g/4oz	(English) walnuts or hazelnuts, chopped	¾ cup
115g/4oz	crystallized lemon peel, chopped (see page 218)	⅔ cup
170g/6oz	stem ginger*, drained and chopped (optional)	1 cup
115g/4oz	dried pears, chopped	⅔ cup
115g/4oz	figs, chopped	⅔ cup
	grated rind of 1 lemon	
	juice of ½ lemon	

1. Cream margarine and sugar until light and fluffy. Beat in eggs gradually, adding a tablespoon of flour if mixture seems likely to curdle.
2. Sieve together flour, salt and baking powder, and fold into creamed mixture. Add remaining ingredients and juice. Mix gently. Put in a greased 20cm/8-inch round cake tin.

3. Bake in a moderate oven at 325°F/170°C/gas mark 3 for 2½–3 hours, covering with greaseproof paper if necessary for the last hour to prevent burning.

Note to Cooks

Crystallized pineapple and lemon peel are obtainable from health food stores and some supermarkets.

CITRUS PEEL FOR CAKES AND PUDDINGS

Gluten Free   Milk Free   Egg Free

Metric/Imperial		American
4 tbs	lemon or grapefruit peel, chopped into small pieces	1 cup
570ml/1 pint	water	2½ cups
1 tbs	sea salt	1 tbs

1. Use undyed fruit if possible. Scrub the skins well.
2. Mix the water and salt and soak the peel in it overnight.
3. Drain and rinse in clear water.
4. Use in rock cakes, fruit cakes, etc. Keeps in the 'fridge for several weeks.

MARZIPAN

Gluten Free   Milk Free   Egg Free

Metric/Imperial		*American*
115g/4oz	cashews, hazelnuts or brazil nuts, ground	¾ cup
1 tbs	clear honey*	1 tbs
½ tsp	natural vanilla essence	½ tsp

1. Mix all ingredients well together. This amount will cover an 20cm/8-inch cake.

Note to Cooks

Can also be used as a cake filling.

NO-SUGAR ICING

Covers a 20cm/8-inch cake or 24 small cakes
Gluten Free   Milk Free   Egg Free

Metric/Imperial		American
115g/4oz	coconut cream	1 cup
2 tbs	boiling water	2 tbs

1. Grate coconut cream, add boiling water and stir until creamy. Smooth over cake with a knife dipped in hot water and leave to set.

Note to Cooks

For carob icing, add 2 tbs carob powder. Add water as necessary.

FUDGE ICING

Covers a 20cm/8-inch cake
Gluten Free   Egg Free

Metric/Imperial		*American*
55g/2oz	unsalted butter	¼ cup
3 tbs	milk	3 tbs
115g/4oz	ground demerara sugar	⅔ cup

1. Combine all the ingredients in a saucepan, and boil gently for ½ minute. Remove from heat and leave to cool. Beat well until thick.
2. Spread over the top of the cake, or slice cake horizontally and sandwich together with the icing.

CREAMY FILLING FOR CAKES AND BUNS

Makes enough for 1 20cm/8-inch cake

Metric/Imperial		American
285ml/½ pint	milk	1⅓ cups
2	egg yolks	2
55g/2oz	ground raw cane sugar	¼ cup
1 level tbs	organic white flour	1 level tbs
15g/½oz	butter	½ oz

1. Put the milk into a saucepan and bring to the boil.
2. Whisk together the egg yolks and sugar until creamy and thick, then gradually stir in the flour.
3. Pour the milk onto the egg mixture, whisking all the time. Put it all back again into the rinsed-out saucepan. Bring to the boil, stirring constantly, and simmer gently for 5–6 minutes, continuing to stir.
4. Take the pan off the heat and beat in the butter.
5. Pour the cream into a bowl and cover the surface carefully with buttered greaseproof paper to prevent a skin from forming. Leave to cool.
6. Store in the 'fridge and use within 3 days.

CAROB YOGURT FILLING

Covers a 20cm/8-inch cake
Gluten Free   Egg Free

Metric/Imperial		American
140ml/¼ pint	thick-set natural (plain) yogurt, or Greek yogurt	⅔ cup
1 tbs	carob powder, sieved	1 tbs
1 tbs	muscovado sugar	1 tbs

1. Combine all the ingredients together and use to sandwich a carob cake. Remember the yogurt will not keep long out of the 'fridge, so the cake needs to be eaten quickly.

CHRISTMAS PUDDING

Makes 2 675g/1½lb puddings
Milk Free

Metric/Imperial		American
55g/2oz	85% self-raising flour	½ cup
½ level tsp	ground cinnamon*	½ level tsp
½ level tsp	ground nutmeg*	½ level tsp
¼ level tsp	ground fennel	¼ level tsp
¼ level tsp	sea salt	¼ level tsp
170g/6oz	figs, finely chopped	1 cup
170g/6oz	dried pears, finely chopped (remove any hard core)	1 cup
85g/3oz	crystallized lemon peel and/or pineapple, finely chopped (see page 218)	½ cup
85g/3oz	raw cane sugar	½ cup
115g/4oz	suet or vegetable fat	½ cup
140g/5oz	fresh wholemeal (wholewheat) breadcrumbs	2½ cups
45g/1½oz	hazelnuts, chopped (no need to skin)	4½ tbs
1 small	carrot, grated	1 small
2	free range eggs	2
1 tbs	black treacle (or molasses*)	1 tbs
2 tbs	strained juice and grated rind of 1 lemon	2 tbs
	water to mix	

1. Sieve flour, spices and salt together and add to fruit, peel, sugar, suet, breadcrumbs, hazelnuts and grated carrot.
2. Beat the eggs and warm the treacle. Add these with the rind and juice of the lemon to the rest of the ingredients. Mix to a dropping consistency with water.
3. Put into two 850ml (1½ pint) oiled pudding basins and cover with a double sheet of oiled greaseproof paper and either a pudding cloth or a layer of foil.
4. Place in a steamer or pan of boiling water to cover ⅔ of the basin.
5. Steam for 5 hours topping up water as necessary. Cool and put clean covers on as before. To serve, reheat for 2 hours.

12

Spreads and Sandwich Fillings

SARDINE PÂTÉ

Gluten Free   Milk Free   Egg Free

Metric/Imperial		*American*
125g/4½oz can	sardines in oil	125g/4½oz can
1	hard boiled egg (free range)	1
1 tbs	lemon juice	1 tbs
	sea salt and freshly ground pepper	
2 tbs	chopped parsley	2 tbs

1. Drain the oil from the sardines and put to one side.
2. Mash the sardines and egg together until you have a smooth paste. Stir in 1 tbs of sardine oil, the lemon juice, pepper and parsley.
3. Taste and add salt if necessary. Cover and chill in the 'fridge.

Serve with hot buttered toast, cress or watercress.

VEGETARIAN PÂTÉ

Another idea for packed lunches or to spread on hot toast for tea.

Gluten Free   Milk Free

Metric/Imperial		American
1 small	onion, chopped	1 small
2 sticks	celery, finely chopped	2 stalks
1	turnip or carrot, finely chopped	1
1 clove	garlic, crushed	1 clove
1 tbs	oil	1 tbs
115g/4oz	cashew nuts, ground	¾ cup
55g/2oz	toasted sesame seeds, ground	½ cup
1 tsp	dried rosemary*	1 tsp
½ tsp	dried thyme*	½ tsp
1 tbs	natural wheat-free soya (soy) sauce (tamari)	1 tbs
	sea salt and freshly ground pepper	
1	free range egg	1

1. Sauté the onion, celery, turnip or carrot and crushed garlic in the oil for a few minutes until soft. Mix with the remaining ingredients and liquidize until smooth.
2. Grease a small ovenproof dish and spoon in the mixture, smoothing the top with a knife.

3. Bake in the oven at 350°F/180°C/gas mark 4 for 40 minutes until firm to touch. Leave to cool in the dish, then turn out on to a plate if required.

HUMMUS

Metric/Imperial		American
115g/4oz	chick peas (garbanzo beans)	½ cup
1 clove	garlic	1 clove
1 tbs	safflower or sunflower oil	1 tbs
1 tbs	sesame paste (tahini)	1 tbs
	juice of a large lemon	
	sea salt	
1 tbs	chopped parsley	1 tbs

1. Soak the chick peas (garbanzos) overnight. Drain, cover with fresh water, and bring to the boil. Simmer until tender for 1–2 hours depending on the batch, or cook in a pressure cooker for 30 minutes.
2. Put the garlic, oil, sesame paste and lemon juice into the liquidizer. Liquidize together then gradually add the chick peas, adding some of the cooking liquid to enable the liquidizer to work. Add sea salt and more lemon juice to taste if necessary. Sprinkle the chopped parsley on the top.

Notes to Cooks

1. If you haven't any sesame paste, grind 1 tablespoon of sesame seeds in a grinder, then mix with safflower or sunflower oil until it is the required thickness.

2. Serve hummus as a dip, using strips of raw carrot or celery. Put it into pitta bread, with lettuce, watercress or cress, or for a good sandwich filling.
3. This freezes well, so you can make a big batch and freeze it. You can also use haricot or butter beans for this recipe.

HOMEMADE TOFU

This is a very versatile food, which can be used in many ways. You can slice it, dip it into flour and fry it, then sprinkle with natural soya (soy) sauce. You can use it in cheesecakes, or in pancakes and cakes, or make it into dips, or mayonnaise.

Gluten Free   Milk Free   Egg Free

Metric/Imperial	*American*
500ml/17.6 fl oz soya (soy) milk carton	2¼ cups
juice of 2 medium-sized lemons	

1. Heat the soya (soy) milk and remove it when it rises in the pan.
2. Stir in the lemon juice, mixing vigorously, and continue to stir for about ½ minute. The milk should now have separated into curds and whey.
3. Pour into a muslin bag and hang to drip for several hours. If you are storing the tofu, it should be kept in water in the 'fridge, and it will keep for about a week like this.

Note to Cooks

Ready-made tofu can be purchased in many health food shops. Choose firm tofu for slicing etc, and silken tofu (soft) for creaming.

VEGETABLE CREAM CHEESE

Gluten Free   Milk Free   Egg Free

Prepare as for Homemade Tofu, adding 2 teaspoons of safflower or sunflower oil to the tofu, then sea salt to taste and you have a tasty cream cheese. For added flavour you can add chopped chives, parsley, celery seed or other herbs. Serve on dry biscuits or in salads.

PEAR BLENDER

This makes a lovely spread and it is much better than jam as it contains less sugar.

Gluten Free   Milk Free   Egg Free

Metric/Imperial		American
455g/1lb	pears	1 pound
115g/4oz	dates*	1 cup
juice of 1	lime	juice of 1
2 tbs	honey*	2 tbs

1. Wash the pears very thoroughly, remove cores, and peel if preferred.
2. Chop the dates and pears roughly.
3. Place in a blender with the lime juice and honey.
4. Blend until the mixture is a thick purée.

Notes to Cooks

Serve as a sweet with equal parts of plain yogurt, or spread on bread or biscuits.
Will keep in the refrigerator for up to 3 days.

HAZELNUT SPREAD

This is a very quick spread to make, providing you have a grinder. Alternatively, ground hazelnuts can be obtained from health-food shops. Ideal if you've run out of ideas for tea. It's packed with protein.

Gluten Free   Milk Free   Egg Free

Metric/Imperial		*American*
115g/4oz	hazelnuts	¾ cup
1½–2 tbs	clear honey* or maple syrup	1½–2 tbs

1. Toast the hazelnuts under the grill for a minute or two, turning frequently as they burn easily.
2. Grind until fine, then mix well with the honey. If the mixture is too thick, thin with a little water.
3. Store in a screw top jar in the refrigerator.

Note to Cooks

For another flavour you can add a tablespoon of carob powder.

SPREADS AND SANDWICH FILLING IDEAS

Meat

1. Chicken or turkey, finely chopped and mixed with a little softened milk free margarine or butter to bind.
2. Chicken, salad cream and Chinese leaves.
3. Turkey, lettuce, cress and salad cream.

Fish

1. Well mashed tinned fish (eg. sardines, tuna, salmon) with a squeeze of lemon juice.
2. Tuna or sardines, lettuce and chopped parsley.
3. Crab and watercress.
4. White fish, fennel and lettuce.

Nuts and Seeds

1. To make a nut spread put chosen chopped nuts in liquidizer, grind and add water to make a spreading consistency. Cashews are good to start with, then get braver and try brazils or hazelnuts.
2. Cashew nut spread and celery.
3. Hazelnut spread and sliced pears.
4. Tahini (sesame spread), lettuce and bean sprouts.
5. Sunflower seed spread, mashed banana and coconut.
6. Sunflower seed spread and chopped figs.

Fruits and Vegetables

1. Mashed banana and chopped nuts.
2. Mashed banana, mixed with a little carob powder.

3. Pear Blender, page 234.
4. Yeast extract and cooked mashed vegetables.
5. Yeast extract, cooked mashed pulses and watercress.
6. Hummus, page 230.
7. Vegetarian Pâté, page 228.
8. Vegetable Cream Cheese, page 233.

Egg

1. Well-mashed hard-boiled egg, with salad cream and cress.
2. Hard-boiled egg, chopped and mixed with mayonnaise and Chinese leaves.
3. Scrambled egg with watercress.

Cheese

Ricotta is soft and white like curd or cottage cheese. It is sometimes made with cow's or goat's milk but the 'real stuff' is made with sheep's milk. It can be flavoured with chopped parsley, chives etc. or sprouted mung beans, permitted chopped nuts, or figs, ground sesame and/or sunflower seeds. Feta cheese is usually made with sheep's milk, but it can also be made with goat's or cow's milk. A fairly hard white cheese, which can be grated.

Etorki is firm and pale yellow, rather like Edam or Gouda. It slices or grates nicely, and is made with sheep's milk.

Goat's milk cheese is like ricotta, or is available as a hard cheese.

Check all cheeses for artificial colours and flavours.

1. Use quark, curd or cottage cheese in place of butter.
2. Cottage cheese, melon or grapefruit with a sprinkling of ginger.*
3. Cottage cheese with pineapple and bean sprouts.
4. Feta cheese and sliced pears.
5. Feta cheese with pineapple.
6. Grated cheese, chutney and bean sprouts or young tender spinach leaves.
7. Grated cheese and spring onions (scallions).

Sandwiches can be toasted in cold weather.

Gluten-free Packed Lunches

Most sandwich fillings can be used (as above) in gluten-free breads. Select your own choice of salad ingredients and pack in tubs.

Sweets/Puddings

These can also be packed in tubs or food flasks. For instance:

1. Fruit – any permitted fresh, stewed or canned, cut up and put in tubs with their own juices or other permitted pure juices. Experiment with flavours to add variety.
2. Millet pudding or ground rice pudding. These can be carried hot in food flasks.
3. Jellies – made in tubs if possible.
4. Flans, crumbles or breads made with permitted grains.
5. Pieces of melon or pineapple.

6. Figs, permitted fruit and/or nut bars. Biscuits and crisps (potato chips) if allowed.
7. Take a selection of nuts and/or seeds – sunflower, sesame and dill seeds are delicious.
8. Permitted cake or biscuits.

KATH'S GRAPEFRUIT MARMALADE

Makes approximately 1,350g/3lb
Gluten Free   Milk Free   Egg Free

Metric/Imperial		American
2 large	grapefruit	2 large
1 large	lemon	1 large
850ml/1½ pints	water	3¾ cups
680g/1½lb	raw cane sugar	4 cups

1. Scrub the fruit, then put into a saucepan with the water. Boil gently with the lid on, for 30 minutes until the fruit is soft.
2. Remove the fruit from the pan, saving the water. Cut in half and scrape out the fruit pulp, pips and some pith, and put in a separate container.
3. Cut the peel to small matchstick-sized strips, or mince it, then put it back into the saucepan with the cooking water.
4. Take the pips and pieces of segment skin and boil in another saucepan with a little water for 15 minutes to release the pectin.
5. Drain and add the water to the shredded peel, with the rest of the fruit pulp.
6. Add the sugar and boil until setting time is reached, usually about 15–30 minutes.
7. Pot and cover with waxed paper. Seal when cold.

FIG AND LEMON PRESERVE

Makes 1.8kg/4lb
Gluten Free   Milk Free   Egg Free

Metric/Imperial		*American*
900g/2lb	dried figs	6½ cups
1,140ml/2 pints	cold water	5 cups
	rind and juice of 4 lemons	
680g/1½lb	raw cane sugar	4 cups

1. Wash the figs, remove stalks, and cut into pieces. Put into a bowl and cover with the water, then leave to soak overnight.
2. Put into a large saucepan or preserving pan, add the strained lemon juice and grated rind, and the sugar.
3. Bring slowly to the boil, stirring to dissolve the sugar, then boil well for 15–20 minutes until setting time is reached.
4. Pour into warm jars while still hot, and cover with waxed paper. Seal when cold.

LEMON CURD

Makes 680g/1½lb (1½ pounds)
Gluten Free

Metric/Imperial		American
2	lemons, scrubbed	2
225g/½lb	raw cane sugar	1⅛ cups
115g/4oz	unsalted butter	½ cup
2	free range eggs	2

1. Put the juice and grated rind of the lemons, the sugar and butter into a basin. Stand in a saucepan of boiling water, or use a double saucepan, and gently heat.
2. While this is heating, beat the eggs and stir into the melted ingredients, then cook gently until mixture thickens. Do not allow the curd to boil. Cool slightly.
3. Pot and cover with waxed paper. Seal when cold. Keep in the fridge.

Note to Cooks

Best eaten within a week.

MELON AND GINGER JAM

Buy the melons when they are at their cheapest, otherwise this could be rather an expensive jam. Choose fruit that is not too ripe.

Makes approximately 1.3–1.8 kilos (2½–3lb)
Gluten Free   Milk Free   Egg Free

Metric/Imperial		American
1 large	melon (approximately 3lb to make 680g/1½lb of fruit when cut away from the skin)	1 large
340g/¾lb	raw cane sugar	2 cups
2 tbs	lemon juice, plus the peel and white pith of the lemon	2 tbs
30g/1oz	bruised root ginger or 1 tsp powdered ginger*	1oz

1. Quarter the melon. Scrape out the pips, cut the fruit away from the skin, and cube.
2. Put into a bowl and cover with the sugar, then leave overnight for the juice to be extracted.
3. Place the pith and peel of the lemon, and the bruised root ginger in a muslin bag.
4. Put the lemon juice and the fruit and sugar mixture in a preserving pan with the muslin bag, and fast boil until setting time is reached. This may be after only 5 minutes. When testing for setting always remove the pan from the heat, otherwise you may boil past setting time.

5. Pot and cover with waxed papers, and seal when cold.

Note to Cooks

Using the same method you can make marrow and ginger jam.

RHUBARB AND LEMON JAM

Makes 900g/2lb
Gluten Free   Milk Free   Egg Free

Metric/Imperial		American
455g/1lb	rhubarb	1 pound
	juice and peel of 2 lemons	
	(scrub skins well)	
455g/1lb	raw cane sugar	2⅔ cups

1. Clean the rhubarb and cut it up into small pieces. Add strained lemon juice. Simmer gently in a saucepan or preserving pan.
2. When the fruit is soft add the sugar and finely chopped lemon peel.
3. Boil fast until setting time is reached. To check this, remove the jam from the heat and drop a little on to a cold plate. Leave until cold then push with finger tip. If setting time has been reached, the jam will crinkle. If this does not happen, boil the jam fast for a few more minutes. Remove scum.
4. Allow to cool slightly then put into clean jars, and put on waxed papers. When cold cover with transparent covers.

PEAR AND CHIVE RELISH

Makes 455g/1lb (1 pound)
Gluten Free   Milk Free   Egg Free

Metric/Imperial		American
455g/1lb	pears	1 pound
225g/½lb	onions	1⅓ cups
285ml/½ pint	distilled white vinegar*	1⅓ cups
170g/6oz	raw cane sugar	1 cup
2 tbs	chopped fresh chives	2 tbs
¼ tsp	sea salt	¼ tsp

1. Wash, core but do not peel the pears, and cut into small dice. Chop the onions into small pieces.
2. Put the pears and onion into a saucepan with the vinegar and cook gently until just soft, about 15 minutes.
3. Stir in the sugar, chives and salt and cook fairly fast for another 40–50 minutes, until thickened.
4. Pot and cover. Serve with cheese and biscuits, or burgers, etc.

13

Special Occasions

PARTY IDEAS

1. Pieces of celery filled with Quark.
2. Cheese and pineapple on cocktail sticks.
3. Half a walnut, and a cube of cheese on a cocktail stick.
4. Mini pizzas (see pizza recipe on page 80).
5. Pizza potatoes – Make a ratatouille topping with one onion, one garlic clove and courgettes (zucchini)*. Spread on a baked potato, add a slice of cheese, and chopped mushrooms. Grill until the cheese melts.
6. Homemade vegetable pasties – Make shortcrust or flaky pastry and fill with cooked mixed vegetables such as onions, carrots, potatoes, celery, turnips, mushrooms and a clove of garlic if liked. Mix with some cooked pulses or cooked rice and vegetable stock and bake.
7. Savoury Rolls (see page 251).
8. Double-decker sandwiches with alternate white and brown slices. Use either the same fillings or two

different ones, such as chopped prawns, mayonnaise and lettuce, cold scrambled egg with mustard and cress.

Crudités

Children seem to enjoy dipping and the slices of vegetables make a healthy colourful addition to the party table. Try serving these vegetables with one of the dips that follow:

Carrots: Cut into thick matchstick shapes, or slice horizontally and cut out shapes with a small biscuit cutter.

Celery: Cut into thin matchsticks.

Radishes: Red or white.

Spring Onions (Scallions): Trim and cut into appropriate lengths.

Turnips: Cut into sticks.

Chinese leaves: Use the thicker white parts nearer to the base.

Pieces of pineapple.

Cauliflower florets.

SESAME DIP

Sesame seeds are an excellent source of calcium.

Gluten Free   Milk Free   Egg Free

Metric/Imperial		*American*
2 tbs	tahini (sesame paste)	2 tbs
1 clove	garlic, crushed (optional)	1 clove
2 tbs	finely chopped parsley	2 tbs
2 tbs	lemon juice	2 tbs
1 tsp	wheat-free tamari (soya sauce)	1 tsp

1. Mix all the ingredients well together. Add 2 tbs water and mix again.

QUARK DIP

Metric/Imperial		*American*
225g/8oz	Quark	1 cup
2 tbs	chopped parsley or chives	2 tbs
	freshly ground pepper	

1. Mix all the ingredients together.

SAVOURY ROLLS

Makes 12 medium

Metric/Imperial		American
115g/4oz	dried butter (lima) beans or 1 430g (15-oz) tin, well drained	⅔ cup
55g/2oz	carrot, grated	½ cup
2 sticks	celery, finely chopped	2 stalks
2 tbs	chopped parsley	2 tbs
	sea salt and freshly ground pepper	
2 tbs	toasted sesame seeds	2 tbs
1 tsp	yeast extract	1 tsp
1	egg yolk, free range egg white for brushing pastry	1

Pastry:

285g/10oz	85% plain flour	2½ cups
140g/5oz	margarine	½ cup + 2½ tbs
2 tsp	lemon juice water to mix	2 tsp

1. Wash the beans and soak overnight.
2. Cook the beans for 1–1½ hours until soft.

3. Mince or mash together with the grated carrot, chopped celery, mixed herbs, sea salt and pepper and sesame seeds.

4. Mix the yeast extract with the egg yolk, then add to the mixture.

5. Make the pastry by rubbing the fat into the flour, and mix in the lemon juice with enough water to form a stiff dough.

6. Roll out into a long strip, and roll the filling into a long strip the same length as the pastry. Place the filling along the middle of the pastry, brush the edges with water, fold over and seal.

7. Brush the top with egg white and cut into 12 medium pieces. Make three small slits in each roll and bake in the oven at 400°F/200°C/gas mark 6 for 25–30 minutes.

TROPICAL PINEAPPLE FRUIT SALAD

Gluten Free   Milk Free   Egg Free

Metric/Imperial		American
1	fresh pineapple**	1
	fruits of choice eg.	
	mangoes, papayas (paw paw),	
	persimmons (sharon fruit),	
	bananas, melon or	
	watermelon, guavas*, figs,	
	pomegranates, grated coconut	

1. Slice the top off the pineapple, hollow out the flesh and place in a mixing bowl.
2. Take out the hard middle core, and any discoloured parts.
3. Cut the pineapple flesh and the fruits of your choice into bite sized pieces and put back into the pineapple shell.
4. Replace the top and serve chilled.

Note to Cooks

If you prefer you could do the same thing using a melon.

** Fresh pineapple is higher in salicylates than canned.

PINEAPPLE AND GINGER
MACAROON GATEAU

The strained Greek yogurt makes a lovely filling, and you can get it made from cow's or sheep's milk.

Serves 6
Gluten Free

Metric/Imperial		American
4	egg whites, free range	4
85g/3oz	ground raw cane sugar	½ cup
115g/4oz	finely ground hazelnuts	¾ cup
1 tbs	rice flour	1 tbs
	rice paper	

For the filling:

225g/½lb tin	pineapple pieces in their own juice, or fresh pineapple pieces*	½ pound can
225g/½lb	strained Greek yogurt (or any thick set yogurt)	1 cup
55g/2oz	chopped crystallized or stem ginger*	2 tbs

1. Turn the oven to 275°F/140°C/gas mark 1. Line one or two large well-oiled baking tins with rice paper.
2. Whisk the egg whites until they are stiff and will form soft peaks. Add two tablespoons of sugar and continue to whisk for about a minute. Gently fold in the rest of the sugar, ground hazelnuts and rice flour.

3. Spread the mixture into three thin circles 15–18cm (6–7 inches) in diameter on the rice paper.

4. Bake in the pre-set oven for 1–1¼ hours until they are crisp, then leave in the switched off oven for an hour to dry thoroughly. Cool and store in an airtight tin.

5. It is best to fill the circles about 2–3 hours before serving, so that they will be soft enough to cut.

6. Fill the circles as you would a gateau. Divide the yogurt into three, then put a layer between each circle adding the pineapple and ginger pieces. Spread the top with yogurt and decorate with the remaining pineapple and ginger pieces.

PROFITEROLES WITH CAROB SAUCE

This recipe uses rice flour and makes deliciously light crisp profiteroles. You can of course use wheat flour if preferred.

Makes about 20
Gluten Free

Metric/Imperial		American
55g/2oz	unsalted butter	¼ cup
140ml/¼ pint	water	⅔ cup
55g/2oz	rice flour	3 tbs
pinch	sea salt	pinch
2	free range eggs	2
140ml/¼ pint	double (heavy) cream or	⅔ cup
225g/½lb	strained Greek yogurt	1 cup

For the sauce:

2 tbs	carob powder, sieved	2 tbs
2 tbs	ground raw cane sugar	2 tbs
2 tsp	oil	2 tsp
2 tbs	water	2 tbs

1. Melt the butter in the water and bring to the boil. Remove from the heat immediately and stir in the flour and salt. Beat with a wooden spoon until a soft ball is formed and the mixture leaves the sides of the pan.

2. Beat in the eggs one at a time, making sure each egg is absorbed before adding the next. The mixture should be smooth and glossy.

3. Put the mixture in large teaspoon-sized balls on to a greased baking tray. Bake in the oven at 350°F/ 180°C/gas mark 4 for 30 minutes. They should be crisp and lightly browned on top.

4. Remove from the oven and slit each one to let the steam escape.

5. Cool on a wire rack.

6. Blend the sauce ingredients together over a gentle heat. Whip the cream if used, and fill the profiteroles with either the cream or yogurt. Spread the sauce on the tops. Can be frozen after adding the cream and sauce.

LEMON SHORTBREAD

Egg Free

Metric/Imperial		American
115g/4oz	butter	½ cup
85g/3oz	raw cane sugar	½ cup
2 tsp	lemon juice	2 tsp
	grated rind of ½ lemon	
115g/4oz	wholemeal (wholewheat or 85%) flour	1 cup
55g/2oz	rice flour	3 tbs

1. Cream together softened butter and sugar. Add juice and rind of lemon, then the flour and ground rice. Rub the mixture together with your fingers until it forms a shortbread dough.
2. Roll it out and cut into fingers. Crimp the ends of the fingers and prick with a fork.
3. Put into a greased baking tin and bake for 30 minutes at 325°F/170°C/gas mark 3. Cool and store in an airtight tin.

CELEBRATION SHORTBREAD

Egg Free

Metric/Imperial		American
140g/5oz	butter	½ cup + 2½ tbs
85g/3oz	raw cane sugar grated rind of 1 lemon	½ cup
55g/2oz	crystallized ginger, chopped fine*	⅓ cup
30g/1oz	cut lemon peel	1 heaped tbs
115g/4oz	wholemeal (wholewheat or 85%) flour	1 cup
115g/4oz	rice flour	¾ cup
30g/1oz	chopped hazelnuts	¼ cup

1. Cream the butter until soft then add the remaining ingredients, except the hazelnuts. Work the mixture together to make a dough.
2. Press into a greased 20cm (8-inch) round cake tin. Crimp the edges and prick all over with a fork. Mark into 8 pieces, and top with chopped hazelnuts.
3. Bake in the centre of the oven at 350°F/180°C/gas mark 4 for 45 minutes until the hazelnuts are golden brown. Remove from tin when cold. This shortbread keeps well in a tin for up to 2 weeks.

FRUITY TRUFFLES

Makes 14
Gluten Free   Milk Free   Egg Free

Metric/Imperial		American
85g/3oz	dried pears	½ cup
85g/3oz	hazelnuts, (English)	⅔ cup
	walnuts or cashew nuts	
30g/1oz	sesame seeds	¼ cup
1 tbs	carob powder, sieved	1 tbs
½–1 tbs	raw cane sugar	½–1 tbs
a little	water or juice	a little
	desiccated coconut to coat	

1. Rinse dried pears in boiling water, then soak in boiling water for 10 minutes.
2. Grind the nuts and seeds.
3. Rinse the pears. Remove cores and mince or mash, then mix with the other ingredients. Bind together with water or juice.
4. Make into small balls, coat in the desiccated coconut, and refrigerate. These make nice nutritious sweet treats for parties.

ICE LOLLIES (POPSICLES)

Gluten Free   Milk Free   Egg Free

Pineapple – Add a few drops of lemon juice to unsweetened pineapple juice to taste. Freeze in ice lolly (popsicle) containers.

Grapefruit – (Makes 2) Squeeze the juice from a grapefruit, and add 2 teaspoons of honey*. You may have to warm the mixture a little to combine the two. Put in ice lolly (popsicle) containers and freeze.

TOFFEE

Gluten Free   Egg Free

Metric/Imperial		American
225g/½lb	demerara sugar	1⅛ cups
115g/4oz	butter (not margarine as it will not work)	½ cup
2 tsp	black treacle (molasses°)	2 tsp

1. Boil ingredients together for 3–6 minutes until a little of the mixture will set when dropped into cold water.
2. Put into a buttered tin and leave to set.

Note to Cooks

2 tablespoons of sesame seeds can be added when setting time is reached to make sesame toffee. Alternatively, add 115g/4oz (¾ cup) of brazil nuts or other nuts like walnuts or hazelnuts.

HOMEMADE CAROB EASTER EGGS

Makes 2
Gluten Free   Egg Free

Metric/Imperial		American
115g/4oz	carob chips, or bars	⅔ cup
2 medium-sized	empty egg shells with a hole in the top	2 medium-sized

For the soft centre:

30g/1oz	ground hazelnuts or (English) walnuts	¼ cup
1 tsp	honey*	1 tsp

1. Put the carob chips or bars into a basin and stand in a bowl of hot water to melt them.
2. Pour the contents of the eggs into a basin through a hole in the top of the egg. Rinse the egg shells. Boil in water for 5 minutes.
3. Mix the nuts with the honey to make two small balls.
4. Stand the egg shells in egg cups and pour the melted carob into the openings until half full. Put in the walnut balls, then the rest of the melted carob. Leave to set.
5. Either serve turned upside down in their shells, pretending they are boiled eggs, or peel and wrap in gold or silver foil, and decorate with flowers.

14

Drinks

T EA AND coffee are stimulants and can be addictive. The following are useful substitutes. Herbal teas and grain coffees are often an acquired taste so persevere. To make drinks more interesting, make a 'pot of tea for one'.

Herbal Teas

These are refreshing and beneficial. They are usually bought packed in tea bags and are made as for ordinary tea. Leave to stand for 10 minutes to infuse. Sweeten if desired with honey* or raw cane sugar.

They should be served without milk.

Try some of the following:

- lime flower
- chamomile
- fennel
- lemon balm (Melissa)
- verbena.

Coffee Substitutes

Most contain some of the following:

- roasted barley
- rye
- chicory*
- oats
- millet
- figs.

Dandelion Coffee

Roasted dandelion root and lactose. Warning: lactose is a form of milk sugar and will affect those with a milk intolerance.

Carob Powder (Chocolate Substitute)

Use in place of cocoa for drinks and cooking. Even additive free pure cocoa contains caffeine, a stimulant.

Yeast Extract

This contains vitamin B_{12}, important for vegetarians. Some brands contain no salt.

Milk

Goat's and sheep's milk may be accepted in cases of cow's milk allergy. Due to their relatively high sodium levels, however, they should not be given to children below the age of one year. They are also low in certain vitamins and minerals so it is essential to seek medical advice if considering using them as an alternative to cow's milk.

Soya Bean Plant Milk (see also page 23)

May be used in drinks. Available in cans or cartons with or without raw cane sugar. It is important to note that soya milks available from supermarkets and health-food shops are *not* fortified with the full range of vitamins and minerals and, as such, are nutritionally incomplete. They are not, therefore, suitable for infants and young children. It is important to contact your doctor or state-registered dietitian if you are considering trying alternative milks and if you think your child is sensitive to cow's milk.

Permitted Fruit and Vegetable Juices

Dilute to taste with hot or cold water, or sparkling mineral water. Or make your own juices with an electric or hand juicer. Concentrated pear juice diluted with sparkling mineral water is particularly nice.

CITRUS FRUIT DRINKS

Gluten Free   Milk Free   Egg Free

1. All drinks can be stored in clean glass bottles. If plastic containers are needed use white lined containers that have no odour. Coloured containers are not advised.
2. HOT DRINKS If drinks are needed hot, put required amount into a strong mug. Place mug in a heatproof basin and pour boiling water into basin. Leave until required heat is reached. This method is better than heating the drink in a saucepan directly over heat.
3. 'FRUIT COCKTAIL' DRINKS Mix any combination of permitted fruit juices together. Add a slice of lemon and ice cubes. Any extra strained juice from permitted stewed fruit can be used, and this makes a good flavoured drink. Stewed, strained fruit juices are also nice on their own.

HAWAIIAN QUENCHER

This is a really refreshing drink.

Serves 2
Gluten Free   Egg Free

Metric/Imperial		*American*
140ml/¼ pint	natural (plain) yogurt	⅔ cup
140ml/¼ pint	pineapple or pear juice	⅔ cup
1 tsp	ground raw cane sugar	1 tsp
	fresh pineapple cubes	

1. Whisk the yogurt, pineapple or pear juice and sugar together until blended. Serve in tumblers with pineapple cubes.

GRAPEFRUIT DRINK

Serves 3–4
Gluten Free   Milk Free   Egg Free

Metric/Imperial		American
2 tbs	raw cane sugar	2 tbs
570–850ml/	boiling water	2½–3¾
1–1½ pints		cups
1	grapefruit	1

1. Stir the sugar into the water and heat until dissolved. Allow to cool then stir in the juice squeezed from the grapefruit.

GRAPEFRUIT AND LIME DRINK

Serves 3–4

Gluten Free   Milk Free   Egg Free

Metric/Imperial		American
2 tbs	raw cane sugar	2 tbs
725–850ml/	boiling water	3–3¾
1¼–1½ pints		cups
½	grapefruit	½
1	lime	1

1. Stir the sugar into the water and heat until dissolved. Allow to cool. Squeeze the juice from the grapefruit and the lime, strain if preferred and add to the mixture.
2. Serve chilled.

LEMONADE

Serves 3–4

Gluten Free   Milk Free   Egg Free

Metric/Imperial		American
2	lemons, medium size	2
2 tbs	raw cane sugar	2 tbs
575–850ml/	boiling water	2½–3¾
1–1½ pints		cups

1. Scrub the skins of the lemons well. Peel the rind thinly, put into a large jug with the sugar and pour over the boiling water.
2. Allow to cool, then add the juice squeezed from the lemons. Serve chilled.

LEMON AND LIME DRINK

Choose limes that are beginning to yellow, as these are juicier and riper than the dark green ones.

Serves 3–4
Gluten Free **Milk Free** **Egg Free**

Metric/Imperial		American
1	lemon	1
2 tbs	raw cane sugar	2 tbs
850ml/1½ pints	boiling water	3¾ cups
1	lime	1

1. Scrub the lemon well. Peel the rind thinly, put into a large jug with the sugar, then pour over the boiling water.
2. Allow to cool, then add the juice squeezed from the lemon and the lime. Chill well before serving.

FRESH LIMEADE

Serves 3–4

Gluten Free   Milk Free   Egg Free

Metric/Imperial		*American*
850ml/1½ pints	water	3¾ cups
2 tbs	raw cane sugar	2 tbs
2	limes	2

1. Heat the water in a saucepan, then stir in the sugar and mix until dissolved.
2. Allow to cool. Squeeze the juice from the limes and add to the mixture. Serve chilled.

LEMON BARLEY WATER

Serves 4–5
Milk Free   Egg Free

Metric/Imperial		American
55g/2oz	pot barley	⅓ cup
2	lemons, medium sized (scrub skins well)	2
850ml to 1.14 litres/1½–2 pints	boiling water	3¾–5 cups
2 tbs	raw cane sugar	2 tbs

1. Wash the barley and slice the lemons. Pour on the boiling water.
2. Cool and add the sugar. Leave to stand overnight or for at least 12 hours for all the goodness to be extracted. Strain.

See also milk shakes and drinks in the Breakfast section, pages 40–41.

Glossary

Salicylates

ASPIRIN SENSITIVITY usually reveals itself as a wheeze when it is taken to relieve pain or fever, though it can also cause rashes and other allergic symptoms. Breathing problems would probably first be noticed an hour or two after taking the aspirin. People who are allergic to aspirin are usually sensitive to the 'acetyl' part of acetyl salicylic acid, though some are sensitive to all salicylates.

Natural salicylate is a substance closely allied to aspirin and which occurs naturally in certain foods. People who are sensitive to aspirin may also have a reaction to these foods.

Several synthetic flavourings used in foods contain a salicylate radical. Salicylates also crop up in chewing gum, soft and fizzy drinks, toothpastes, mouthwashes, suntan lotions, lozenges, ice creams, jams and jellies.

Salt of Benzoic Acid

This is a white crystalline organic acid produced commercially from petro chemicals, and used as an antiseptic and preservative, and in certain types of dyes. It occurs naturally in peas, pineapple and cranberries.

Antioxidant

This is a substance added to oils and fats to stop them going rancid when exposed to oxygen in the air. Ascorbic acid (vitamin C) and the tocopherols (vitamin E family) both have antioxidant properties.

The synthetic antioxidants B.H.A. (butylated hydroxyanisole) and B.H.T. (butylated hydroxytoluene) are widely used as antioxidants for animal fats. These are excluded in the Feingold Diet.

Coeliac Disease

A disease in which damage to the lining of the intestine prevents the body from absorbing important nutrients. Symptoms are loss of weight, diarrhoea with offensive stools full of undigested fat, stomach pain, and sometimes vomiting. These symptoms are caused by an intolerance of gluten, a protein found in wheat, barley, rye and oats. Medical advice must be sought if you think your child is suffering from this condition to ensure correct diagnosis and full dietary advice.

Essential Fatty Acids

The essential fatty acids are linoleic and alpha linolenic acid. They are called essential as they cannot be manufactured by the body. These fatty acids are found in vegetable and seed oils particularly safflower, sunflower and corn oil. Although expensive, cold pressed oils are better as these have not been heated during refining.

Studies suggest that a number of hyperactive and allergic children may be unable to metabolize essential fatty acids because of inhibited enzyme activity (which may occur through faulty diet or illness), or lack of sufficient linoleic acid in the diet or the necessary co-factors (zinc, magnesium, B vitamins and vitamin C) needed for the conversion of linoleic acid to Prostaglandin E.1.

Prostaglandin E.1. appears to be important in the control of the immune system – behaviour – kidneys – thirst – asthma – eczema. A recent study confirms the connection made by Sally Bunday and Vicky Colquhoun of the Hyperactive Children's Support Group (HACSG) that hyperactive children have lower concentrations of essential fatty acids in their body. Many hyperactive children appear to suffer from excessive thirst and have low levels of zinc.

For more information on essential fatty acids as a supplement, research paper and parents' notes write to the Secretary, HACSG at the address on page 12. Please send 75p in stamps and a 20 x 25cm stamped addressed envelope.

Special Diets

IDEAS FOR GLUTEN-FREE
AND MILK-FREE MEALS

Breakfast

Grapefruit and Melon
   Refresher
Soya (Soy) Yogurt
Hazelnut Milk Shake

Soups

Everything Soup
Carrot and Lemon Soup
Watercress Soup
Leek and Potato Soup

Main Meals (*Note:* Beef may be a problem for those allergic to milk)

Lamb and Swede
   (Rutabaga) Loaf
Rabbit Casserole
Roast Lamb with Garlic
   and Rosemary
Shish Kebab
Gluten-free Dumplings
Lemon Chicken
Carrot and Potato Loaf
Special Savoury Lentils
Homemade Tofu
Beefburgers
   (Hamburgers)
Salmon Kedgeree

Salads

Bean Salad
Carrot Salad
Beansprout and Cashew

Nut Salad
Green Salad
Melon and Prawn Salad
Cauliflower Salad
Coleslaw

Puddings

Fresh Fruit Salad
Mango Tofu Surprise
Soya (Soy) Crumble
Rhubarb Jelly
Pineapple Jelly
Baked Marzipan Pears
Banana Sweet
Instant Lemon Pudding
Nut Cream
Tofu Whipped Cream
Basic Sponge/Pudding
  (recipe under bread
  and cake section)

Bread and Cakes

Potato Bread Yeast Free
Basic Sponge/Pudding
  recipe
Coconut Pyramids
Hazelnut Macaroons
Sunflower/Sesame Bars
Citrus Peel for Cakes and
  Puddings

Marzipan
No Sugar Icing

Spreads

Sardine Pâté
Vegetarian Pâté
Hummus
Vegetable Cream Cheese
Pear Blender

Sandwich Fillings

See section.

Jams and Chutneys

See section.

Sweets, Parties, Special Occasions

Sesame Dip
Tropical Pineapple Fruit
  Salad
Iced Lollies (Popsicles)
Fruity Truffles

Drinks

See section.

IDEAS FOR GLUTEN-FREE MEALS

Breakfasts

Grapefruit and Melon
  Refresher
Fruit Breakfast Yogurt
Yogurt
Soya (Soy) Yogurt
Millet Porridge
Banana and Lemon
  Health Drink
Hazelnut Milk Shake

Soups

Everything Soup
Cauliflower Soup
Minestrone
Carrot and Lemon Soup
Watercress Soup
Leek and Potato Soup

Main Meals

Salmon Kedgeree
Lamb and Swede
  (Rutabaga) Loaf
Bubble and Squeak
Rabbit Casserole
Roast Lamb with Garlic

and Rosemary
Lemon Lamb Meatballs
Shish Kebabs
Gluten-free Dumplings
Lemon Chicken
Rice and Cheese Savoury
Chinese Rice
Stir Fry Vegetables in a
  Sweet & Sour Sauce
Carrot and Potato Loaf
Brussels Sprouts with
  Chestnuts
Potatoes Sesame Style
Special Savoury Lentils
Lentil Roast
Homemade Tofu (recipe
  under Spreads)
Lamb/Beefburgers
  (Hamburgers)

Salads

Banana Salad
Rice Salad
Bean Salad
Carrot Salad
Beansprout and Cashew
  Nut Salad
Green Salad

Melon and Prawn Salad
Melon, Ginger and Curd
   Cheese Salad
Cauliflower Salad
Coleslaw

Puddings

Fresh Fruit Salad
Fig and Yogurt Dessert
Mango Tofu Surprise
Instant Mango Delight
Instant Banana Whip
Rhubarb Fool
Rhubarb Jelly
Pineapple Jelly
Baked Marzipan Pears
Pear 'Clafoutis'
Banana Sweet
Butterscotch Bananas
Coconut Supreme
Instant Lemon Pudding
Chestnut Delight
Mango Meringue Pudding
Millet Milk Pudding
Baked Custard
Caramel Custard
Custard Sauce
Nut Cream
Tofu Whipped Cream
Yogurt Ice Cream

Carob Ice Cream
Basic Sponge/Pudding
   (recipe under Bread and
   Cakes)

Bread, Cakes and Pastry

Potato Bread Yeast Free
Gluten Free Pastry
Gluten-free Baking
   Powder
Soya (Soy) Crumble
Gluten Free Biscuits
Basic Sponge/Pudding
   Recipe
Coconut Pyramids
Hazelnut Macaroons
Sunflower/Sesame Bars
Citrus Peel for Cakes and
   Puddings
Marzipan
No Sugar Icing
Fudge Icing
Carob Yogurt Filling
Butter Filling or Topping

Spreads

Sardine Pâté
Vegetarian Pâté
Hummus

Vegetable Cream Cheese
Pear Blender

Sandwich Fillings

See section.

Jams and Chutneys

See section.

Sweets, Parties and Special Occasions

Sesame Dip
Quark Dip
Pineapple and Ginger

Macaroon Gateau
Profiteroles with Carob
  Sauce
Tropical Pineapple Fruit
  Salad
Iced Lollies (Popsicles)
Sunflower/Sesame Bars
Fruity Truffles
Toffee
Homemade Carob Easter
  Eggs

Drinks

See section.

IDEAS FOR MILK-FREE MEALS

Breakfasts

Grapefruit and Melon
  Refresher
Crunchy Muesli with
  Soya (Soy) Milk
Soya (Soy) Yogurt
Oatmeal Porridge
Millet Porridge with Soya
  (Soy) Milk
Hazelnut Milk Shake

Soups

Everything Soup
Minestrone
Carrot and Lemon Soup
Watercress Soup
Leek and Potato Soup

Main Meals

Salmon Kedgeree
Casserole of Beef
Lamb and Swede
  (Rutabaga) Loaf
Rabbit Casserole

Roast Lamb with Garlic
and Rosemary
Shish Kebab
Gluten-free Dumplings
Liver Lyonnaise
Lemon Chicken
Fish Fingers (Sticks)
Tuna and Cod Fish Cakes
Cauliflower Fritters
Chinese Rice
Stir Fry Vegetables in
Sweet and Sour Sauce
Vegetable Crumble
Carrot and Potato Loaf
Celebration Nut Roast
Special Savoury Lentils
Baked Beans
Homemade Tofu (recipe
under Spreads)
Turkey Burgers
Lamb/Beefburgers
(Hamburgers)
Pasta Nests
Liver Goujons with Pasta

Salads

Rice Salad
Bean Salad
Carrot Salad
Beansprout and Cashew

Nut Salad
Pasta Salad
Green Salad
Melon and Prawn Salad
Cauliflower Salad
Coleslaw
Homemade Salad Cream
French Dressing

Puddings

Fresh Fruit Salad
Mango Tofu Surprise
Soya (Soy) Crumble
Rhubarb Jelly
Pineapple Jelly
Baked Marzipan Pears
Carob Pear Pudding
Banana Sweet
Instant Lemon Pudding
Custard/Milk Pudding
Nut Cream
Tofu Whipped Cream
Basic Sponge/Pudding
(recipe under Bread and
Cake section)

Breads and Cakes

Potato Bread Yeast Free
Homemade Wholemeal
Bread

Basic Sponge/Pudding
  recipe
Coconut Pyramids
Sunflower/Sesame Bars
Hazelnut Macaroons
Crunchie Cookies
Christmas Pudding
Citrus Peel for cakes and
  puddings
Marzipan
No Sugar Icing

Spreads

Sardine Pâté
Vegetarian Pâté
Hummus
Vegetable Cream Cheese
Pear Blender

Sandwich Fillings

See section.

Jams and Chutneys

See section.

Sweets, Parties and Special Occasions

Sesame Dip
Tropical Pineapple Fruit
  Salad
Iced Lollies (Popsicles)
Fruity Truffles

Drinks

See section.

IDEAS FOR EGG-FREE MEALS

Breakfasts

Grapefruit and Melon
  Refresher
Alpine Breakfast
Crunchy Muesli
Fruity Breakfast Yogurt
Yogurt
Soya (Soy) Yogurt
Oatmeal Porridge

Millet Porridge
Parsnip or Swede
  (Rutabaga) Fritters
Banana and Lemon
  Health Drink
Hazelnut Shake

Soups

Everything Soup
Cauliflower Soup
Minestrone
Carrot and Lemon Soup
Watercress Soup
Leek and Potato Soup

Main Meals

Herrings in Oatmeal
Casserole of Beef
Rabbit Casserole
Roast Lamb with Garlic
    and Rosemary
Lemon Lamb Meatballs
Shish Kebab
Cottage Pie Bake
Dumplings
Liver Lyonnaise
Lemon Chicken
Tuna and Cod Fish
    Cakes
Baked Fish in Yogurt
    Sauce
Stir Fry Vegetables in
    Sweet and Sour Sauce
Pasta Nests
Chicken Lasagne
Potatoes Sesame Style

Vegetable Crumble
Vegetable Pie
Brussels Sprouts with
    Chestnuts
Special Savoury Lentils
Baked Beans
Homemade Tofu (recipe
    under Spreads)
Lamb/Beefburgers

Salads

Rice Salad
Bean Salad
Carrot Salad
Beansprout and Cashew
    Nut Salad
Green Salad
Melon, Ginger and Curd
    Cheese Salad
French Dressing
Pasta Salad

Puddings

Fresh Fruit Salad
Fig and Yogurt Dessert
Soya (Soy) Crumble
Mango Tofu Surprise
Pear and Mango Crumble
Date and Nut Slice

Rhubarb Jelly
Pineapple Jelly
Banana Sweet
Butterscotch Bananas
Millet Milk Pudding
Nut Cream
Tofu Whipped Cream
Yogurt Ice Cream
Carob Ice Cream

Breads, Cakes and Pastry

Homemade Wholemeal
  Bread
Shortcrust Pastry
Sesame Thins
Yogurt Scones
Sunflower and Sesame
  Bars
Flapjacks
Oat Crunchies
Crunchie Cookies
Gingerbread Men
Ginger Biscuits
Citrus peel for Cakes and
  Puddings
Marzipan
No Sugar Icing
Fudge Icing
Carob Yogurt Filling

Spreads

Sardine Pâté
Hummus
Vegetable Cream Cheese
Pear Blender

Sandwich Fillings

See section.

Jams and Chutneys

See section.

Sweets, Parties and Special Occasions

Sesame Dip
Quark Dip
Tropical Pineapple Fruit
  Salad
Carob Bars
Iced Lollies (Popsicles)
Fruity Truffles
Lemon Shortbread
Celebration Shortbread
Toffee
Homemade Carob Easter
  Eggs

Drinks

See section.

Useful Addresses

AAA (Action Against Allergy), 24/26 High Street, Hampton Hill, Middlesex TW12 1PD. Tel: (0181) 943 4244.

AIA (Allergy Induced Autism), 3 Palmera Avenue, Calcot, Reading, Berkshire RG3 7DZ. Tel: (01734) 419460.

Association for Breastfeeding Mothers, 26 Hernshaw Close, London SE26 4TH. Tel: (0181) 788 4769.

Asthma Society, 300 Upper Street, London N1 2XX. Tel: 0345 01 02 03 (1–9pm).

BDA (British Dietetic Assoc.), 7th Floor, Elizabeth House, Suffolk Street, Queensway, Birmingham B1 1LS. Tel: (0121) 643 5483.

British Dyslexia Association, 98 London Road, Reading, Berkshire RG1 5AU. Tel: (01734) 668271.

Coeliac Society, PO Box 220, High Wycombe, Bucks. HP11 2HY. Tel: (01494) 437278.

Department of Health, Richmond House, 79 Whitehall, London SW1. Tel: (0171) 210 5983/3000.

Food Commission (Consumer Watchdog on Food), 3rd Floor, 5–11 Worship Street, London EC2A 2BH. Tel: (0171) 628 2442 Fax: (0171) 628 9329.

Foresight (Assoc. for Preconceptual Care), Old Vicarage, Church Lane, Witley, Goldalming, Surrey GU8 5PN.

Health Visitors' Association, 50 Southwark Street, London SE1 1UN. Tel: (0171) 378 7255.

Henry Doubleday Research Association, Ryton-on-Dunsmore, Coventry CV8 3LG. Tel: (01203) 303517. Research on growing organic food.

HACSG (Hyperactive Children's Support Group), Sally Bunday, 71 Whyke Lane, Chichester, West Sussex PO19 2LD. Tel: (01903) 725182.

La Leche League (Breastfeeding Help), BM 3424, London WC1N 3XX. Tel: (0171) 242 1278.

Mencap, 123 Golden Lane, London EC1Y 0RT. Tel: (0171) 454 0454.

MAFF (Ministry of Agriculture Fisheries and Food),
Nobel House, 17 Smith Square, London SW1P 3HX.
Tel: (0171) 238 3000.

National Association of Toy and Leisure Libraries, 68
Church Way, London NW1 1LT. Tel: (0171) 387
9592. Have a database of toy libraries throughout the
country where hyperactive children can have access to
a wide range of toys. A magazine, *The Good Toy Guide*, is
available on request.

National Autistic Society, 276 Willesden Lane, London
NW2 5RB. Tel: (0181) 451 1114.

National Childbirth Trust, Alexandra House, Oldham
Terrace, London W3 6NH. Tel: (0181) 992 8637.

National Eczema Society (NES), 163 Eversholt Street,
London NW1 1BU. Tel: (0171) 388 4097.

National Play Bus Association, 93 Whitby Road,
Brislington, Bristol BSA 3KF. Tel: (0117) 977 5375.

National Society for Research into Allergy, PO Box 45,
Hinckley, Leics. LE10 1JY. Tel: (01455) 851 546/
291294.

Research Trust for Metabolic Diseases in Children,
Golden Gates Lodge, Weston Road, Crewe, Cheshire
CW1 1XN. Tel: (01270) 250221.

Soil Association (Organic Food Regulatory Body), 86
Colston Street, Bristol BS1 5BB. Tel: (0117) 929 0661.

RECIPES FOR HEALTH

Irritable Bowel Syndrome

JILL DAVIES AND ANN PAGE WOOD

Irritable Bowel Syndrome, or IBS, is a very common bowel disorder which accounts for over 50 per cent of referrals to gastro-intestinal clinics. What you eat is of great importance in helping to control this condition.

Specialists usually advise a high-fibre diet – and many sufferers benefit from a diet low in fat and high in protein.

This practical guide can be used in conjunction with your doctor's treatment. The authors:

- explain what is meant by the term 'irritable bowel syndrome'
- discuss the various physical and psychological factors associated with the disorder
- give guidelines on coping with IBS

The tempting recipes are based on cereals, fruit and vegetables, and high-protein foods. The amount of fibre is given in each dish.

With this book, you can help yourself to better health and learn to cope with and even overcome your IBS.

RECIPES FOR HEALTH

Diabetes

Low fat, low sugar, carbohydrate-counted recipes for the management of diabetes

AZMINA GOVINDJI AND JILL MYERS

This imaginative cookbook is also a comprehensive guide to living with diabetes, containing practical information as well as a delicious range of over 100 recipes carefully devised for a diabetic diet. It includes easy, everyday meals, meals for two, recipes to entertain with, ideas for cooking for children, vegetarian meals, tempting desserts and much more.

Each recipe is coded for calories and carbohydrate content. The recipes are ideal for anyone wanting a healthy low fat, high fibre, low sugar diet.

| RECIPES FOR HEALTH: IBS | 0 7225 3141 9 | £5.99 | ☐ |
| RECIPES FOR HEALTH: DIABETES | 0 7225 3139 7 | £5.99 | ☐ |

All these books are available from your local bookseller or can be ordered direct from the publishers.

To order direct just tick the titles you want and fill in the form below:

Name: _____

Address: _____

_____

_____ Postcode: _____

Send to: Thorsons Mail Order, Dept 3, HarperCollins*Publishers*, Westerhill Road, Bishopbriggs, Glasgow G64 2QT.
Please enclose a cheque or postal order or your authority to debit your Visa/Access account –

Credit card no: _____

Expiry date: _____

Signature: _____

– to the value of the cover price plus:
UK & BFPO: Add £1.00 for the first book and 25p for each additional book ordered.
Overseas orders including Eire: Please add £2.95 service charge. Books will be sent by surface mail but quotes for airmail despatches will be given on request.

24 HOUR TELEPHONE ORDERING SERVICE FOR ACCESS/VISA CARDHOLDERS – TEL: 0141 772 2281.